BRITAIN IN OLD PH

ILKLEY

PAST & PRESENT

ALEX COCKSHOTT & DENISE SHILLITOE

SUTTON PUBLISHING

Sutton Publishing Limited
Phoenix Mill · Thrupp · Stroud
Gloucestershire · GL5 2BU

First published 2005

Copyright © Alex Cockshott and Denise
Shillitoe, 2005

Title-page photograph: Aerial view of Ilkley,
showing the Cow and Calf Rocks.
(Denise Shillitoe)

British Library Cataloguing in Publication Data
A catalogue record for this book is available from the
British Library.

ISBN 0-7509-3922-2

Typeset in 10.5/13.5 Photina.
Typesetting and origination by
Sutton Publishing Limited.
Printed and bound in England by
J.H. Haynes & Co. Ltd, Sparkford.

H.M. Collins and his orchestra at the Kings Hall Annex, 1927. *(Denise Shillitoe)*

CONTENTS

The Grove, looking east. *(Bradford Museums, Galleries and Heritage)*

Key for Map

1   To Myddelton Lodge
2   Oak Ghyll
3   Low Hall
4   Stubham Rise
5   The Old Bridge
6   Lido
7   New Bridge
8   Roman fort site, Manor House,
    All Saints' Church
9   Old Grammar School
10 Heathcote
11 To Heber's Ghyll
12 Thorpe Hall/Arden Lea
13 St Margaret's Church
14 Westwood Lodge
15 Wells House
16 Hillside
17 Rombald's Hotel
18 Troutbeck
19 Craiglands
20 Ilkley Grammar School
21 Library, Town Hall, King's Hall
22 Railway Station
23 Operatic House
24 Waterworks
25 Wheatley Hall
26 St John's
27 Ben Rhydding Methodist
    Church
28 The Wheatley
29 Ben Rhydding Hydro (site)
30 Cow and Calf Hotel

Map of Ilkley.

INTRODUCTION

Ilkley is situated in the valley of the River Wharfe, about 16 miles west of Leeds and 14 miles north of Bradford. A trunk road, the A65, runs through the town, heading for Skipton and the Yorkshire Dales beyond. Ilkley lies on the boundary of West Yorkshire and North Yorkshire. The town straddles the river: on the south side lie the nineteenth-century developments and the shopping and business area; on the north side lies the twentieth-century residential area of Middleton.

Occupation of the moors that overlook Ilkley took place long before people lived in the valley bottom. The moors are scattered with the remains of prehistoric cairns and barrows. Artefacts such as stone axes and worked flint tools are regularly found. The moors are famous internationally for their concentration of carved rocks, referred to as 'cup and ring' rocks. There are over three hundred of these. Many are now covered in vegetation, but some have been well known since Victorian times. Examples are the 'Swastika Stone', situated on the edge of Woodhouse Crag, and the Hangingstone Quarry rock, which can be found just to the west of the Cow and Calf Rocks. Their purpose is unknown, but theories abound.

The Romans arrived in AD 79–80, engaged in subduing the local tribes. The locality is well situated for defence and communication and the river is fordable. They built a timber fort with turf ramparts on a small mound overlooking the river, with streams running down the west and east sides. The east stream, now culverted,

'Swastika' stone.
(*Denise Shillitoe*)

West wall of the Roman fort. (*Alex Cockshott*)

Crosses, Ilkley churchyard.   Roman wall and manor house. *(Denise Shillitoe)*
(Denise Shillitoe)

still flows beneath Brook Street. The fort was subsequently rebuilt in stone. All that
remains today is a small fragment of the west wall.

A civilian settlement grew up to the south of the fort and this provided the
beginnings of the village of Ilkley. Little is known about this phase of Ilkley's
development, nor, indeed, when the name Ilkley was first used.

There was undoubtedly a Christian church established sometime before the
Norman Conquest. Three Anglo-Saxon crosses still remain, dated to the ninth
century. They form part of a local style of sculptured crosses, other examples of
which are found in Leeds and Collingham. The crosses used to stand outside All
Saints Church, but were moved inside the church in 1983 to protect them from
pollution and further weathering. A church is mentioned in the Domesday Book,
which also records that half the manor was wooded and the rest was uncultivated
pasture or wasteland. All Saints Church was built within the site of the Roman fort:
much of the stone used in its building is reused Roman stone. The tower and doorway
arch date from the fifteenth century, but the remainder of the structure is Victorian.

Apart from the parish church, one of the oldest surviving Ilkley buildings is the
Old Castle, now known as the Manor House, which is also sited within the old fort.
Very little of its early history is known. Architecturally, it is a medieval building with
a screen passage. Parts are sixteenth century, but it has been extensively remodelled
over the years. After restoration in the 1950s it opened as the Manor House Art
Gallery and Museum. The history of the building features in Chapter 1.

Following the Norman conquest the manor of Ilkley belonged to the de Percy
family. During the fifteenth century ownership of the land passed to the Middeltons,
whose main residence was Stockeld, near Wetherby. It remained in this family until
parcels of land were sold in the late nineteenth and early twentieth centuries. The
name of Middleton is still to be found in many local roads and buildings. The district
of Middleton and the history of Myddelton Lodge form the subject of Chapter 3. The
spelling of Middleton is confusing, as many different spellings have been used over
the years. We have used Middelton as the family name, Middleton as the district and
Myddelton for the area where the family lived, as this is the most accurate.

During the Civil War the Middelton family were recusants (that is, they were Catholic at a time when Catholicism was forbidden) and Royalists. William Middelton, the Lord of the Manor, was at the sieges of Skipton and Pontefract Castles. Despite a series of fines and land confiscations, the family managed to keep the majority of the estate intact until the nineteenth century.

During the late eighteenth and early nineteenth centuries Ilkley was a small, impoverished agricultural village, confined to the area covered by the modern Church Street and Brook Street. Brook Street took its name from the fact that the stream, Mill Ghyll, ran down the road until it was culverted. The grassy banks were covered with wild flowers in the summer. There were three crossing places – parapet bridges at the top and bottom and a clapper bridge in the middle.

The cottages in Ilkley were usually of one storey with thatched roofs. The majority of the occupants were involved with farming in some way. Unlike in Addingham and Burley, the villages either side of Ilkley, the textile industry never developed here. This was largely because the Middeltons did not wish to have their view from Myddelton Lodge spoilt by industry.

A growing belief in the healing power of bathing meant that by the mid-eighteenth century it had become popular to 'take the waters' at various spa towns in England and on the continent. Perhaps surprisingly in view of its lowly status, Ilkley had had a bath house since 1690 at White Wells which was visited by people living in the north. In the early 1840s the Lord Mayor of Leeds, Hamer Stansfeld, visited a hydrotherapy establishment at Grafenberg in Silesia, run by Vincenz Priessnitz, who had developed 'the water cure'. This involved immersion in cold water combined with energetic physical activity. In 1843 Hamer Stansfeld persuaded a Dr Antoine Rischanek to come to Ilkley to practise hydropathy. He was accommodated in West View and advocated the use of the baths at White Wells (see pages 96 and 97). In 1844 Hamer Stansfeld built a hydro at Wheatley, a small hamlet just east of Ilkley which was named Ben Rhydding Hydro. Today the village of Wheatley is known as Ben Rhydding. Chapter 10 deals with this.

Ben Rhydding Hydro was followed twelve years later by the opening of Wells House Hydro in 1856 and in quick succession by others, including Craiglands in 1859, the Troutbeck in 1863 and the Grove Hydropathic in 1864.

By the mid-nineteenth century Peter Middelton, the Lord of the Manor, was in financial difficulties and began to sell small portions of land. His son William Middelton held the first major sale of land in 1867. This was followed by more sales over the ensuing years, initially confined to the south side of the river.

The release of this land, along with the arrival of the railway in 1865 (and the extension of the railway to Skipton in 1888), meant that Ilkley became an attractive place not only to visit but also to live. By 1871 villas were being built for the merchants and businessmen of Leeds and Bradford. The sale of Middelton land was accompanied by strict conditions set down by the surveyor Joseph Smith, of Bradford. For example, all properties had to have a stone boundary wall built within twelve months of completion and the widths of the roads were specified. The architect of many of these early villas, George Smith, helped to give Victorian Ilkley its distinctive

The top of Brook Street, *c.* 1850
(Denise Shillitoe)

Cottages on Skipton Road, *c.* 1860.
(Denise Shillitoe)

appearance. Several of the architects who designed Ilkley, including George Smith, Charles Henry Hargreaves, James and Edward Critchley, all chose to live in Ilkley.

Following these land sales the old thatched properties began to disappear. With the increase in visitors many of the new houses began to offer accommodation. Development north of the river began during the Edwardian period when the continuing financial straits of the Middelton family required the sale of more land. The majority was bought by a consortium of businessmen known as the Wharfedale Estate Company. On the one hand this led to the development of modern Middleton (Chapter 3), but on the other it led to the loss of woodland. Matters could have been a lot worse if several individuals had not purchased a large number of the plots of land which later came under the ownership of Ilkley Urban District Council. This preserved the area known as Middleton Woods, which is now a Site of Special Scientific Interest.

Ilkley is a residential town. Many visitors still come for a day out to experience what earlier generations came for: clean and bracing fresh air, with the moors, woods and riverside to provide physical activities. The long-distance footpath, the Dales Way, starts at the Old Bridge. There is still a good variety of shops in the town.

This book aims to show the history of modern Ilkley from its beginnings as a health resort through to the present day. Fortunately for local historians there were several photographers in Ilkley who recorded local buildings, local life and current events. They included Albert Anning, Jesse Bontoft, John Buck, John Milner, William Scott and John and Ernest Shuttleworth. Photographs reveal far more than just the visual history of a community. They also tell the story of cultural and economic changes. So, for example, over time hydros became hotels and large private villas became private schools. As the age profile of the population changed many of these became nursing homes. In their turn, nursing homes became less profitable and many closed. As owners struggled to afford the staff and to maintain their properties, the grounds of many large homes and hotels were sold for development. More recently, the explosion in house prices has seen the demolition of several otherwise perfectly serviceable large houses, to be replaced by high-density accommodation. The equation of profit, amenity and quality of life is difficult to balance. Who knows what changes the next hundred years will bring?

1

Church Street

Wheat Sheaf Hotel and All Saints Church, *c.* 1930. The Wheat Sheaf was one of the oldest public houses in Ilkley, owned by the Middelton family until 1880. In 1822 the victualler was Thomas Wharton and according to the tithe map of 1847 the occupier was Thomas Barnes. In the 1890s William Stephenson advertised that 'the dining room [was] 46 feet by 19 feet and would accommodate 100 people, being the largest and most convenient room for balls, picnics, teas and dinner parties in Ilkley'. In 1959, when the public house finally closed, it was owned by Bentley's Brewery who transferred the licence to a new public house, the Wharfedale Gate on Leeds Road. The Wheat Sheaf was demolished in the 1960s. *(Bradford Museums, Galleries and Heritage)*

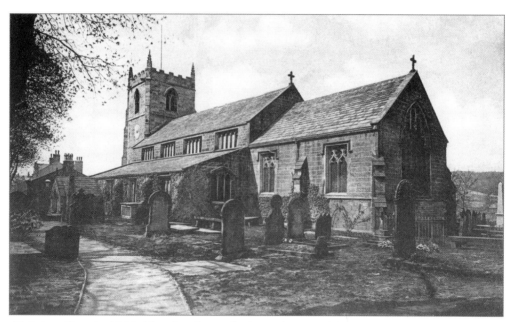

All Saints Church, 1900. The church was built on the site of the headquarters building of the Roman fort. It is likely that there has been a church here since the seventh century: one is mentioned in the Domesday Book. Parts of the north wall are medieval and the tower was added in the fifteenth century. The church was enlarged in 1860, at a cost of £1,300. The roof was removed, the south wall knocked down and rebuilt 10ft nearer to the road, and the nave was extended by 16ft. The thirteenth-century dogtooth moulded archway was retained and rebuilt at the south entrance. *(Denise Shillitoe)*

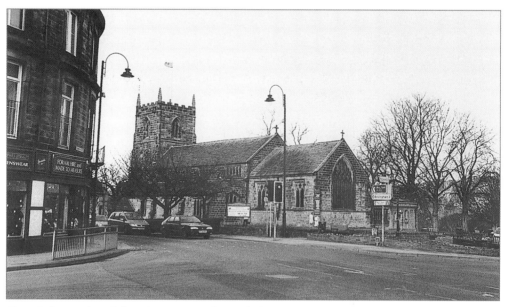

Church Street viewed from junction with Brook Street, 2005. In 1967–8 the gravestones were removed from around the church. This was part of Ilkley Urban District Council's improvement scheme for the area following the demolition of the Wheat Sheaf Hotel. A few of the stones remain against the wall of Church House. The choir vestry and side chapel built in 1927 can be seen to the right of the church. *(Denise Shillitoe)*

Rose & Crown Hotel, *c.* 1860. This was a coaching inn on the turnpike road from Leeds to Skipton. The coach journey from Leeds to Ilkley took about two hours. The hotel was one of the properties offered for sale in July 1869 as part of the fifth Middelton land sale. It was advertised as 'the old established and well-accustomed hotel and posting house with stabling, coach house, sheds, brew-house, outbuildings, garden and yard and also the hairdressers shop; in the occupation of William Kendall and his under tenant and containing 1,928 square yards there about'. *(Bradford Museums, Galleries and Heritage)*

Rose & Crown Hotel, 2005. The original building (seen in the previous photograph with the woman standing outside) was demolished in the 1890s and replaced with a new building. It was designed by Samuel Jackson, who designed several properties for the Ilkley Brewery. *(Denise Shillitoe)*

The Old Castle, *c.* 1865. This picture was taken from Church Street, looking through the archway that leads into Castle Yard. The old house, built on part of the site of the Roman fort, dates mainly from the seventeenth century although there are some fourteenth- and fifteenth-century features. In the 1841 census many of the occupants were described as wool-combers. This was the only area in Ilkley where any occupation connected with the wool trade is known to have taken place. It was included in the Middelton land sale of 1869 and sold to a Mr Watson of Bradford for £850. The house at this time was divided into five cottages. (*Bradford Museums, Galleries and Heritage*)

Castle Yard. This picture shows how the building was split into different cottages. The building on the right is probably an eighteenth-century addition. The young women are standing at the doorway to Mrs Robinson's Refreshment Rooms. (*Sally Gunton*)

The castle viewed from the graveyard, *c.* 1920. *(Bradford Museums, Galleries and Heritage)*

Manor House, 2005. In the 1920s it was suggested that the building should become a museum. Forty years later, on 8 July 1961, Percy Dalton presented the castle to the Ilkley Urban District Council. He had purchased the property in 1941. It was then four cottages and a workshop. By 1955 the cottages had been condemned as unfit for human habitation and Mr Dalton in conjunction with the Council converted the property and renamed it the Manor House. Today the museum has a small display on the history of Ilkley, including the cup and ring rocks and the Roman fort. The upstairs gallery has a regularly changing programme of exhibitions. *(Denise Shillitoe)*

Parade on Church Street, *c.* 1890. The tower of All Saints Church is clearly seen on the left. At the top of the picture the old Star public house is visible and on the right stands the porch of the old vicarage. (*Bradford Museums, Galleries and Heritage*)

Waddington's Refreshment Rooms after the flood, 1900. This old property, which can be seen behind the three leading men in the previous picture, has a date stone of 1709 above the door. For many years it belonged to the Cunliffe family. In the latter half of the nineteenth century the house was split into two shops and the building was later occupied by Woods' Dairy. This picture was taken on the morning after a thunderstorm hit Ilkley on Thursday 12 July 1900. (*Bradford Museums, Galleries and Heritage*)

Church Street, *c.* 1920. Another view of the north side of Church Street, showing the tall three-storey building built in 1895. In 1901 it was a confectioner's and a registry office for servants. In later years it became Stones' Dairy. (*Bradford Museums, Galleries and Heritage*)

Church Street, 2005. The fish and chip shop has become Glovers Garage. The 1709 building has been restored to one property – the Mallard Inn. Church Street forms part of the A65 that runs through the heart of Ilkley, and it is only in the early morning that it is empty of traffic. (*Denise Shillitoe*)

Old vicarage and Charity Hole. This was the vicarage until the 1840s, when the Revd Mr Snowdon arrived. He decided it was too ruinous to live in and had a new vicarage built on Wells Road (Skelda Grange). The porch on the front was erected in the 1770s and became known as the Charity Hole. This was where medicine and fees for the charity baths at White Wells were distributed to the poor and needy. *(Denise Shillitoe)*

Skipton Road and Church Street, *c.* 1900. Another view of Church Street, taken from Skipton Road. The cottage on the right is the Box Tree Restaurant, which in Victorian times was a farmhouse. It first opened as a restaurant in 1962, although previously it had been 'Ye Old Box Tree Café' specialising in home-made cakes and biscuits. The building on the left housed two shops owned by James Robinson Feather: a grocery, and a glass and china business. *(Denise Shillitoe)*

Church Street, *c.* 1930. The Charity Hole was demolished when the Dean Brothers built the Arcade in 1895. The ground floor consisted of shops with a billiard hall above. In 1953 the Arcade was used to hold a party for about fifty children to celebrate the coronation of Queen Elizabeth II. *(Denise Shillitoe)*

Skipton Road and Church Street, 2005. Feather's shops were demolished prior to 1953 and the area was opened up and grassed. *(Denise Shillitoe)*

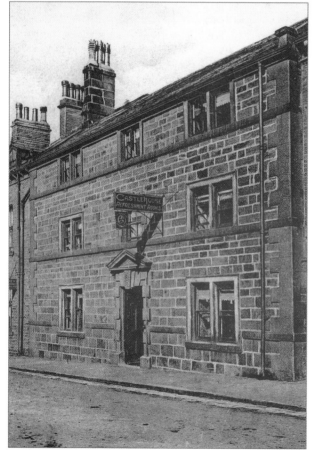

Donkey Jackson's cottage, Bridge Lane. For many years 'Donkey' John Jackson hired out donkeys to take people up the steep incline to White Wells. He was a bell-ringer at All Saints Church. Here he is standing outside his home in Bridge Lane. One of the advertisements on the notice-board is for a concert at Wells House. The roof of the cottage collapsed in 1904 and he moved to a cottage in Castle Yard. *(Denise Shillitoe)*

Castle House, Bridge Lane. Almost opposite Donkey Jackson's house stands Castle House, an early eighteenth-century building. Originally called Low House, it was the farmstead of the Beanland family for many years. At the time of this photograph it had become refreshment rooms and had been renamed Castle House, probably because of the proximity of the castle (now the Manor House Art Gallery and Museum). *(Bradford Museums, Galleries and Heritage)*

Bridge Lane, *c.* 1920. Bridge Lane was the way to the Old Bridge. *(Bradford Museums, Galleries and Heritage)*

Bridge Lane, 2005. The steps on the left of the picture are all that remain of Donkey Jackson's cottage. Castle House, the three-storey building on the right with the prominent windows, has been divided into two houses with an extra door inserted. *(Denise Shillitoe)*

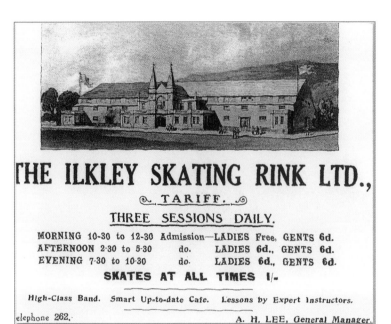

Advertisement for Ilkley's skating rink, *c.* 1902. *(Bradford Museums, Galleries and Heritage)*

West Yorkshire Road Car Company Ltd depot, South Hawksworth Street. This building started life as the roller-skating rink. It later became the bus depot for the West Yorkshire Road Car Company. The small garage next to the depot housed Roy Cunliffe's motorcycle business. On the left, in the foreground, can be seen the corner of the Constitutional Club, built by Isaac and Thomas Dean and opened at the end of the 1890s. *(Ilkley Civic Society)*

The Moors shopping centre, 2005. The bus company remained on the site until the 1980s. The building was then demolished and the Moors shopping centre built. *(Denise Shillitoe)*

2

Skipton Road

The circus parade, Bolton Bridge Road and Skipton Road junction. A visit by the circus, especially Lord George Sanger's, provided a popular entertainment in Ilkley and youngsters were given a half-day's holiday from school. To signal their arrival, the performers would parade through the town en route to the show ground, which was at Yew Croft just off Chapel Lane. The horses in this picture are seen turning off Skipton Road into Bolton Bridge Road. The houses on the left are at the bottom of Yewbank Terrace, built in 1874. They had landscaped communal gardens at the front. *(Bradford Museums, Galleries and Heritage)*

Lister's Arms Hotel. Originally called the New Inn in 1825 when it first opened, it soon became known as the Lister's Arms after the first tenant John Lister. The wing on the far left was at one time used as a brewhouse. The wing on the right is a later addition. *(Denise Shillitoe)*

Lister's Court, 2005. In 1989 the owner of the Lister's Arms sold it to a developer, who converted the original hotel into apartments. The wing on the right was rebuilt and further apartments built on the old car park and gardens. It is now known as Lister's Court. *(Denise Shillitoe)*

Roy Cunliffe's motorbike shop, 1980s. Roy Cunliffe moved his business to this site when his premises in South Hawksworth Street were demolished to make way for the development of the Moors shopping centre. Roy Cunliffe was a well-known motorcyclist who won sidecar races in the 1960s. (*Bradford Museums, Galleries and Heritage, Hilda Holmes*)

Skipton Road, 2005. Roy Cunliffe has moved and there have been several subsequent occupants. Next door is the long-established Mann's Bakery. The bread is baked on the premises at the back. (*Denise Shillitoe*)

Junction of Skipton Road and Alexandra Crescent, *c.* 1897. The presence of flags and bunting suggests that this picture was taken at the time of Queen Victoria's jubilee. It shows the houses and shops on Skipton Road. At the bottom of the road on the right Box Tree Cottage can be seen. The shop in the foreground belonged to a watch- and clockmaker. *(Bradford Museums, Galleries and Heritage)*

Junction of Skipton Road and Alexandra Crescent, 2005. The low garden wall seen in the last picture is still here, but the railings have gone and a hedge has been planted. The shops and houses remain. The one in the foreground is an antique shop and the one adjacent to it is a bookshop. *(Denise Shillitoe)*

The old grammar school, *c.* 1900. This building was erected in about 1637 and was used as the village school until its closure in 1872, when the National School opened on Leeds Road. By the time it closed it was in a poor state of repair. Its position was unsuitable, being close to the highway and having no playing fields. The standard of tuition was also said to be poor. By the time this photograph was taken, the building had been taken over and renovated by the Christian Brethren for use as a chapel. For many years the old grammar school has been an antique-silver shop. *(Bradford Museum, Galleries and Heritage)*

The old grammar school, 2005. *(Denise Shillitoe)*

Demolition of the railway arches, Bolton Bridge Road, 1973. After the closure of the railway line to Skipton in 1965 the track was removed gradually. The railway bridge over Bolton Bridge Road was taken away in 1973. *(Mr Hardisty)*

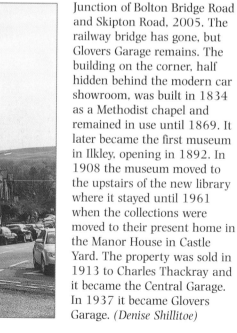

Junction of Bolton Bridge Road and Skipton Road, 2005. The railway bridge has gone, but Glovers Garage remains. The building on the corner, half hidden behind the modern car showroom, was built in 1834 as a Methodist chapel and remained in use until 1869. It later became the first museum in Ilkley, opening in 1892. In 1908 the museum moved to the upstairs of the new library where it stayed until 1961 when the collections were moved to their present home in the Manor House in Castle Yard. The property was sold in 1913 to Charles Thackray and it became the Central Garage. In 1937 it became Glovers Garage. *(Denise Shillitoe)*

Railway arches, Bolton Bridge Road. The railway arches that spanned the area behind Regent Road were used as workshops. They were demolished when the railway line was removed in 1973. *(Bradford Museums, Galleries and Heritage)*

Site of the railway arches, 2005. The area once occupied by the arches became the car park for Bridge House, which forms part of Bradford College. *(Denise Shillitoe)*

Regent Road. This is the end house on the north side of Regent Road, built in the 1890s. The railway viaduct with one of the workshops beneath the arches is clearly visible. *(Denise Shillitoe)*

Regent Road, 2005. A small block of flats has been built next to the end of the terrace. The modern property that can be seen beyond the terraced houses is part of the Lister's Court development. *(Alex Cockshott)*

Flood damage, Chapel Lane, July 1900. During the afternoon of 12 July 1900 a major thunderstorm occurred over Ilkley. The rain was so heavy that many houses were flooded and sustained structural damage. The worst damage was caused by the streams that drained the moors, which were blocked with branches and rocks. Backstone Beck, Mill Ghyll and Parish Ghyll were the main streams that burst their banks, causing over £100,000 worth of damage to property in Ilkley. This picture shows the damage caused by Parish Ghyll Beck in Chapel Lane. It was here that Mr Brogden's coach-making workshop collapsed, killing Alfred, one of Mr Brogden's sons. At the height of the flood the depth of the waters reached 6ft. *(Bradford Museums, Galleries and Heritage)*

Chapel Lane, 2005. In 2005 only the tall house and the one next to it remain. The other properties have been demolished. The area on the left where the car is parked was where Mr Brogden's workshop stood and was later the Wharfedale Creamery. *(Denise Shillitoe)*

North face of Middelton Hotel. Erected in the 1870s, and designed by George Smith, the hotel opened and was named, with permission of the Middelton family, as the Middelton Hotel. It stood on an embankment overlooking the River Wharfe with views over Middleton. Originally not very successful, it later became a popular family hotel offering billiards, tennis, croquet, bowls and fly-fishing. It was also a well-attended venue for local functions. The Ilkley Urban District Council held a banquet here for a hundred townsmen after the opening of the Town Hall complex in 1908. During the Second World War it was used as an Officer Cadet Training Unit and by the War Office Intelligence School. *(Denise Shillitoe)*

Middelton Hotel and Middleton Villas, before 1888. This photograph, taken before the railway was built to Skipton, shows how green and open Ilkley once was. Middelton Hotel dominates the foreground. The small house to the right of the hotel was Stonebank, built in 1874 for Charles Illingworth and later occupied by the Sisters of the Holy Cross and Passion until they moved to Elmleigh. Stonebank was on the south side of Skipton Road, on the corner of Westville Road. The house was demolished in the 1950s. The pair of semi-detached houses next to the hotel was designed by George Smith in 1876 and forms part of Middleton Villas. The house with the turret behind the hotel is Ferndale and behind that is St John's, designed by Norman Shaw. The other large house to the right is Woodbank, later demolished. Wells House stands on the extreme left. *(Denise Shillitoe)*

Ilkley Moor Hotel, 1968. In 1947 Middelton Hotel changed its name to Ilkley Moor Hotel. It became popular with visiting rugby football teams, especially from Australia and New Zealand. In 1968 a fire broke out in the lounge, killing four people and injuring another five. The building was demolished in 1970. *(Bradford Museums, Galleries and Heritage, Hilda Holmes)*

Site of the hotel, 2005. Town houses and apartments have been built on the site. All that remains of the hotel is the bar on Stockeld Road, known locally as the Taps. *(Denise Shillitoe)*

Paradise Gardens, Bridge Lane. These are two views of Paradise Gardens, a small park between the Old Bridge and the Bridge Hotel. On the 1847 tithe map the field was known as Paradise. It later became known colloquially as Tittie Bottle Park because it was popular with nannies and their charges. The top picture shows the Middelton Hotel on the left, and the bottom picture shows the Old Bridge. *(Denise Shillitoe)*

3

Middleton

Boating on the River Wharfe by the Old Bridge, 1905. The bridge was built in about 1675 to replace a previous one which had been washed away by floods in 1673. It provided the only access to Middleton until the New Bridge was built in 1904 – the rowing boats would have been hired from Wray's Pleasure Gardens on the south side of the river in Bridge Lane. In addition to boating, the facilities included a museum, an aviary and a menagerie with monkeys, armadillos, lemurs and racoons. Septimus Wray also owned the Bridge Hotel and organised band competitions and other entertainments. In 1903 he sold the Pleasure Gardens to Mr Garratt, but bought them back in 1912. Ilkley Council purchased the Bridge Hotel in 1936.
(Denise Shillitoe)

Stubham Rise viewed from the Old Bridge, 1899. These houses in Stubham Rise were among the first to be built in Middleton, by the Dean Brothers at the turn of the twentieth century. (*Bradford Museums, Galleries and Heritage*)

Stubham Rise viewed from the Old Bridge, 2005. The main changes that have taken place are the closure of the bridge to vehicular traffic, in 1948, and the building of further houses. (*Denise Shillitoe*)

Low Hall, *c.* 1870. Low Hall is one of the oldest properties in Ilkley. It was the demesne farm for the Middelton family. The room over the porch was reputed to have been used as a chapel by the family, who were devout Catholics. By the 1870s the farmhouse had been divided into two. Mr and Mrs Alderson, who lived in one part, can be seen at their doorway near a large walnut tree. *(Denise Shillitoe)*

Low Hall, 2001. Low Hall was sold in the 1920s and became a private house. The old farm buildings were demolished and the stone used to lay out new gardens. This picture was taken on an Ilkley Civic Society walk in 2001. *(Denise Shillitoe)*

Myddelton Lodge, *c.* 1925. The lodge is a prominent landmark on the hillside on the north side of the river overlooking Ilkley. It belonged to the Middelton family from the twelfth century, first as a hunting lodge, then as a dower house and home. The Middeltons were the Lords of the Manor, although their main residence was at Stockeld near Wetherby. In 1904 the Lodge was sold to Sidney Kellett, a Bradford merchant. After his death in 1920 it was sold to the Passionist Fathers and became St Paul's Retreat, known locally as the Monastery. The building on the left was the chapel that Peter Middelton built in 1825. It was used by the local Catholic community until the new church was opened in Stockeld Road in 1878. *(Denise Shillitoe)*

Myddelton Lodge, 2005. In 2000 the lodge was sold. The wing on the right is the Victorian extension, which has been converted into a separate home – Myddelton House. The left-hand wing with the lancet windows is no longer the chapel and has been converted back to a private house. *(Denise Shillitoe)*

Pastoral and Ecumenical Centre, Myddelton Lodge, 1998. The Passionist Fathers remained at
the lodge until 1985. This plain-looking building was built to provide extra accommodation in
1968. The Roman Catholic Diocese of Leeds took over the complex in 1985. *(Denise Shillitoe)*

Myddelton Grange, 2005. The Diocese of Leeds demolished the old residential complex shown
in the previous photograph and had this new building built further back. *(Denise Shillitoe)*

Oak Ghyll, Langbar Road, *c.* 1905. Oak Ghyll was designed by Perkin & Bulmer, a Leeds-based firm of architects, for C.A. Rickard of Leeds in 1900. It was one of the first large villas to be built in Middleton. The house is at the junction of Langbar Road and Ghyll Bank Road. The 2-acre gardens reached down to Rupert Road. By the 1960s Oak Ghyll had become a convalescent home. *(Denise Shillitoe)*

Oak Ghyll Convalescent Home, Langbar Road, *c.* 1960. *(Denise Shillitoe)*

Oak Ghyll, Langbar Road, 2005. In 1970 Oak Ghyll was sold and converted into apartments. In common with many other large houses with extensive grounds, the land was sold separately for residential development. *(Denise Shillitoe)*

Officer Training Corps Camp, West Holmes Field, Denton Road, 1912. Septimus Wray, the owner of the Pleasure Gardens, initially rented and then in about 1912 purchased the two fields known as the Holmes on the north side of the river. He had a bridge of barrels for pedestrian access built across the river and laid a cycle track on one of the fields. A common sight in Ilkley during the summer months was a tented army camp pitched on the East or West Holmes Field. The writer of this postcard commented that he was 'feeling very fit and we march off for a 20-mile march and bivouac somewhere on the moors, taking firewood, waterproof sheets, great coats and rifles, then at about 2am we may have an attack of some sort'. The houses behind the tents are on Denton Road and were built in the first decade of the twentieth century by Dean & Mennell, a firm of local builders. *(Denise Shillitoe)*

West Holmes Field, 2005. West Holmes Field is still used for recreational purposes, with football a popular weekend activity. The Edwardian houses in the previous picture are clearly identifiable, although further development has taken place. *(Denise Shillitoe)*

Ilkley Lido, *c*. 1935. After a particularly hot summer in 1934 it was decided to build a local swimming pool. Work proceeded quickly and the opening took place in May 1935. A large proportion of the pool was kept shallow enough for young children. There were several water slides and the diving board was of international standard. The café was designed by A. Skinner, Surveyor to Ilkley Council, and was run by C.E. Taylor & Co. of Harrogate, who also owned the Kiosk and Imperial Cafés on The Grove. (*Bradford Museums, Galleries and Heritage*)

Ilkley Lido, *c*. 1950. Looking south towards Ilkley Moor, this picture shows how crowded the Lido became during the summer months. The large, castle-like building centre left was the retort house at the gasworks on Leeds Road, later the site of Booth's supermarket. It was built in 1935 and praised for its proportions. It was in use until the 1960s. (*Denise Shillitoe*)

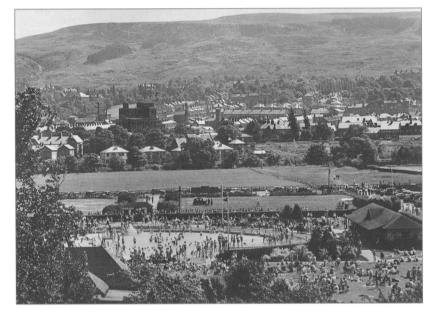

Ilkley Lido and indoor swimming pool, 2005. An indoor swimming pool was opened in 1974 in the grounds of the lido. This was one of the last projects of the Ilkley Urban District Council before it was amalgamated with Bradford Metropolitan Council. (*Denise Shillitoe*)

The New Bridge, looking east, 1905. When the Wharfedale (Ilkley) Estate Co. started to develop Middleton it realised that a new river crossing was desirable. Before then the only local crossing suitable for vehicles had been the Old Bridge. The New Bridge was completed in 1905 but the commemorative plaque wrongly records it as 1904. The official opening was in June 1906. The building on the far right was the Ilkley Working Men's Hall, which was built in 1875 and later became the Liberal Club. The large double-gabled building next to it was originally built as a convalescent home. Later it became an orphanage for girls, where Miss Spruce the matron educated the girls for domestic service. *(Denise Shillitoe)*

The New Bridge looking east, 2005. In 1938 the local dramatic society, the Ilkley Players, began to rent rooms in the Liberal Club. In 1960 they purchased the whole property and it became the Playhouse. Since then there have been several extensions. The orphanage was converted into flats and the roof line has been altered by the addition of dormer windows. The moor and the Cow and Calf Rocks are visible on the skyline. *(Denise Shillitoe)*

Old gasworks and the back of the old Star Inn. Taken from behind the old Star and Wharfedale Inns and the houses on Leeds Road, this shows the stream that flowed down Brook Street from Mill Ghyll, running from the centre of the picture to the left. It also served as a sewer. The tall square chimney was all that remained of the gasworks, which had opened in 1857. The curved roof of the Crescent Hotel can be seen against the moor. (*Bradford Museums, Galleries and Heritage*)

New Brook Street, looking north, 2005. Looking the other way down New Brook Street, this shows the long vista over the New Bridge. The gabled building on the right was designed by Edward Critchley and built by Dean & Mennell in 1909. To the left of the picture was the entrance to the rear of the Wheat Sheaf Hotel. It was here that the annual sheep fair and feast week were held in September. It remained the site of the fair until the 1950s. After the Wheat Sheaf Hotel was demolished the area was turned into gardens and parking space. (*Denise Shillitoe*)

4

Brook Street

Etching looking north down Brook Street, *c.* 1800. At one time there were three small
bridges over the open brook which flowed down the eastern side of the street and
joined the River Wharfe. The carriageway was on the western side. In the early
nineteenth century the thatched cottages along the brook had midden heaps, which
caused the curate Revd George Fenton to campaign for improvements. The brook was
culverted in the 1850s. This is why the road is so wide today. *(Denise Shillitoe)*

Brook Terrace with Hawksworth's Farm, *c.* 1868. Brook Terrace was a purpose-built group of four shops with houses above, constructed in 1855 for Sarah Beanlands. On the left of the shops is a farmhouse. Its last occupant was Billy Hawksworth, who gave his name to the Hawksworth Streets. The farmhouse was demolished to make way for Gothic House in 1869. At the right end of the terrace is John Shuttleworth's shop. Shuttleworth came from Silsden to set up a gift-selling business in 1851, and sold fancy goods, guides and postcards of local views. In 1861 he established the *Ilkley Gazette*, which was published every Saturday. It cost a penny and included the latest list of visitors to Ilkley. The curved wall on the far left is the Crescent Hotel, built in the 1860s. *(Denise Shillitoe)*

Brook Terrace and the former Gothic House, 2005. Brook Terrace is on the right of the picture. Gothic House – with matching gables – is on the left. George Mott had a china shop here in the 1920s and '30s. Later it was a thrift store and in the 1980s the Fish Dish. Over the years the shops have had many different retailers and the ground-floor windows have changed considerably. *(Denise Shillitoe)*

Gothic House: 'The place to buy your gifts.' Following the success of his first shop, John Shuttleworth built Gothic House in 1869 to be the largest shop in Ilkley and to be 'architecturally unique'. He published the *Ilkley Gazette* from here and it also contained his gift-selling business. His son Ernest was his main photographer. Mrs Shuttleworth also worked in the shop while her sister kept house for the family. To the right is the shop of Mr Earnshaw, watchmaker, jeweller and silversmith, established in 1870. He made decorated commemorative keys for the Revd Robert Collyer when he opened the public library in 1907 and for Mr J.T. Jackson when he opened the Town Hall in 1908. *(Bradford Museums, Galleries and Heritage)*

Brook Street, 1862. On this Shuttleworth postcard the cottages at the top of Brook Street are Lister's Refreshment Rooms. These had been demolished by 1870 to widen the junction when Green Lane began to develop as The Grove. One house on the left has changed to a shop. The corner on the right is Brook Terrace. *(Denise Shillitoe)*

The Crescent Hotel and the east side of Brook Street, *c.* 1880. To the left, at the junction with Leeds Road, is the Crescent Hotel. It was built for £8,000 and opened in 1860 as a commercial hotel. Like most of Ilkley's buildings it was built from stone quarried on Ilkley Moor. It had stables and a bowling green. In 1867 the first of the Middelton land sales was held here. *(Bradford Museums, Galleries and Heritage)*

Looking south up Brook Street, *c.* 1880. By this time, as the village had expanded, most of the houses on the left had become shops. On the right is Thomas Critchley's draper's shop. In the top centre is a block of nine shops and houses built for the Leeds and Yorkshire Building Co., designed by Thomas Ambler and built in 1870. *(Bradford Museums, Galleries and Heritage)*

Looking south up Brook Street, *c.* 1906. The metal girder bridge was built in 1888 to carry the railway line extension to Skipton. Behind it is the spire of the Wells Road Wesleyan Church which opened in 1870 – the spire was added in 1876. The church was described as a 'handsome building in the early Gothic style'. The White Wells bath houses can be seen in the distance below the moor edge. On the right are the Brook Terrace shops and Gothic House. The glass veranda belonged to Johnson's Refreshment Rooms, built at the end of the 1890s. *(Denise Shillitoe)*

Looking south up Brook Street, 2005. The railway girder bridge has gone. It was removed on Sunday 10 July 1966. The line to Skipton was closed in 1965 as part of the Beeching Cuts. *(Denise Shillitoe)*

Steamroller on Brook Street, *c.* 1890. Ilkley Local Board's steamroller has fallen through the road into the culvert. Behind it is a coffee tavern. This later became the Wharncliffe Restaurant, which extended at first-floor level into the cottages behind to accommodate some two hundred diners. John Thwaites was a hairdresser and tobacconist selling 'Fancy goods, etc. foreign & British cigars'. *(Bradford Museums, Galleries and Heritage)*

Bottom of Brook Street, 2005. There is a selection of shops on this busy street with cars parked alongside. Although the ground-floor façade has changed over time, the first floor is much as it was. *(Denise Shillitoe)*

Queen Victoria's Diamond Jubilee, 1897. The shops are decorated with bunting to celebrate the jubilee. On the corner with the veranda is William Andrew Johnson's shop – confectioner's, refreshment rooms, beer and wine retailer. He sold Ilkley Wells toffee in souvenir tins. To the left are the shops of Thomas Critchley, draper and silk merchant; Thomas Pell, hosier and draper; and William Lawson, plumber. *(Bradford Museums, Galleries and Heritage)*

West Brook Street, 2005. W.A. Johnson had left by the 1920s and after many changes, including The Gateway, Silvio's Café and The Honest Lawyer, the premises are once more called Johnsons – a café bar. The rest continue to be shops, often with flats or offices above. Critchley's became a bank, which later absorbed Pell's. *(Denise Shillitoe)*

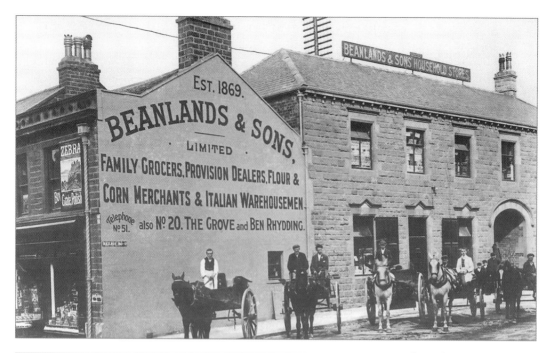

Corner of Brook Street and Railway Road, *c.* 1890 and *c.* 1960. Joseph Beanlands' gable end marks the point where two further shops were demolished in the 1880s when the railway line was extended across Brook Street. A further seventeen houses were demolished along Railway Road as part of that project. In 1895 the archway was added leading to Beanlands' newly built warehouses. By the 1960s the shop had become Monkman's. The large wall on the right is the abutment for the railway. *(Bradford Museums, Galleries and Heritage)*

Corner of Brook Street and Railway Road, 2005. Though the name and the type of shop have changed many times, the outline of this building is the same. *(Denise Shillitoe)*

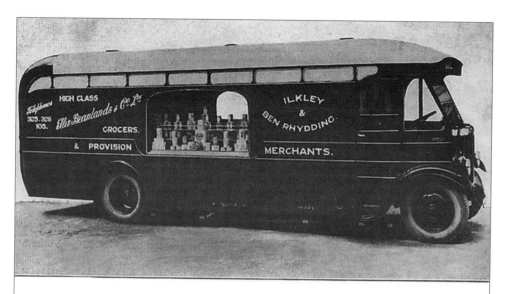

THE
TRAVELLING GROCER

Although designed principally to meet the needs of customers in outlying districts, this latest addition to our service has become so popular that we are compelled to include all districts, near or far, in "The Travelling Grocers" journeys. Everything sold from this modern shop is the usual high class quality and we would esteem it a favour if you will take advantage of this convenient method of shopping.

ELLIS BEANLANDS
AND COMPANY LIMITED
ILKLEY : BEN RHYDDING

Advertisement for Ellis Beanlands, 1930s. The Beanlands family had grocery shops on The Grove, Brook Street, in Ben Rhydding and in the Arcade on Church Street. The one in the Arcade was their last shop, which remained open until the 1970s. (*Denise Shillitoe*)

The Station Hotel in the mid-1880s. On the west of Brook Street buildings were demolished for the railway extension, including the Station Hotel. This had been a coaching inn, with stables built by William Dobson and run by his son Francis. It changed its name to the Station Hotel in 1865 when the railway arrived. Richardson's boot shop is the building being demolished. *(Denise Shillitoe)*

Site of Station Hotel, 2005. After the railway bridge was demolished in 1966 the resultant space was used in the 1980s to build three shops along Brook Street. *(Denise Shillitoe)*

End of Railway Road in the 1980s and Station Plaza, 2005. At the end of the 1980s the railway abutments and some buildings including the Pickfords travel shop were demolished. The side tunnel entrance to the station from Railway Road was blocked off. The Station Plaza shops were built around the 1930s Woolworth store. *(Denise Shillitoe)*

Brook Street, looking north, 1871. On the left are some newly built shops including a chemist's and Boocock, bathmaker and ironmonger. The tall gabled shop was built for John Dobson in 1870, designed by Thomas Marshall. At the bottom, facing up the road, are the Wheat Sheaf and the Star. *(Denise Shillitoe)*

Brook Street, *c.* 1910. This picture shows how the 1888 railway bridge dominated Brook Street. On the left of the photograph, on the corner with The Grove, are a series of shops: Mason's butcher and Arthur Duckworth, chemist (later Boots); and then Yorkshire House with H.J. Rose & Co., drapers (later Busby's). The gabled building had been butcher Thomas Grunwell's, but by 1907 was a branch of the Yorkshire Penny Bank. Next door, another gable, is a branch of the Bradford Old Bank. That bank was built in 1889 to a design by James and Edward Critchley. At the left end of the bridge Ellis Ingham, coal merchant, had built an office. In the foreground people are sitting on the seats round the fountain at the bottom of Mill Ghyll, sometimes referred to as 'the monkey rack'. *(Denise Shillitoe)*

This fountain was built by public subscription in 1875 for £130. When not frozen, water flowed from the nostrils of four horses with further jets around the base. The upper part was surrounded by serpents and mermaids. Water for the fountain came from Mill Ghyll, named after the two corn mills formerly higher up the beck. William Middelton leased Mill Ghyll to the Ilkley Board for one shilling per year in 1873, to be preserved as 'an arboretory with a clear and rippling stream'. The Board planted trees to develop the ghyll as a promenade and it acquired ownership of it in 1893 as part of the purchase of Ilkley Moor from Charles Middelton. (*Bradford Museums, Galleries and Heritage*)

Floral fountain, top of Brook Street. During the Second World War the protective railings were removed from the fountain. This led to vandalism and finally the fountain itself was removed in 1959. The empty stone bowl has been used for a floral display since 1994. (*Denise Shillitoe*)

Oakbridge House, The Wells Walk, *c.* 1890. William Dean had this house built on the west side of Mill Ghyll in 1875. It is in a style popular in Ilkley: an 'L'-shaped semi-detached house on a junction with doorways on different streets. The Deans lived here and let some of the house as apartments including to the curates of St Margaret's Church. William Dean had become the Ilkley Registrar of Births and Deaths by 1901. Dolly Dean can be seen standing in the doorway looking across Hospital Walk towards the moor. For many years the house was a nurses' home. By 2005 it had become a family home. *(Denise Shillitoe)*

Oakbridge House, 2005. *(Alex Cockshott)*

5

The Grove

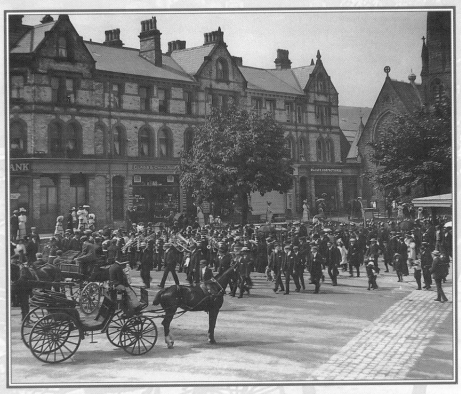

Parade along The Grove. (*Bradford Museums, Galleries and Heritage*)

Hartley's Farm' *c.* 1867. The Grove was originally called Green Lane. It started to be developed piecemeal in the late 1860s and '70s. This old farm building (one of only two on Green Lane) is sometimes known as 'the old Manor House', although there is no evidence that it had ever been the manor house. It was demolished in 1868 to make way for a block of shops with flats above. *(Bradford Museums, Galleries and Heritage)*

Site of 'the old Manor House', 2005. The new buildings, designed by Thomas Ambler, were built using cream Tadcaster brick, which, although attractive, was not of good quality. Originally they housed a variety of retail businesses. In 1901 the building on the right corner was Miss Vaux's refreshment room and confectioners. Next door was M. Sapwell & Co., an art embroidery supplier. It advertised that it stocked all the needs for embroidery and ribbon work as well as offering lessons in ecclesiastical and artistic decoration. At the left corner was the Yorkshire Penny Bank and next to that a hairdresser and tobacconist. Now the premises are occupied mainly by banks and estate agents. *(Denise Shillitoe)*

The Grove, looking west, *c.* 1912. On the left can be seen the properties built to replace Hartley's farm. Beyond them can be seen the tower of the Congregational Church which opened in June 1869. Designed by the architect J.P. Pritchett, it cost over £6,000, much of this sum being raised by subscription. Among the subscribers were Sir Titus Salt of Saltaire. The clock was given by T.P. Muff in 1881 to celebrate his seventieth birthday. The shops opposite were built for Mr Moon, a butcher, in 1871. The veranda was added in the 1880s and two further shops in 1899, on land which had housed Mr Moon's slaughterhouse. *(Bradford Museums, Galleries and Heritage)*

The Grove, looking west, 2005. During the Second World War the railings disappeared from around the gardens – a victim of the 'war effort'. The church is now known as Christchurch, having joined with the Methodist and United Reformed Churches in 1981. *(Denise Shillitoe)*

Nos 10/12 The Grove, 1920. Occupying premises on the north side of The Grove was Dinsdale and Co. The nature of their business is clearly announced by the large sign. They were also the proprietors of the 'Swastika' brand of ancient liqueur whisky, named after the well-known cup and ring marked rock on Ilkley Moor. The architect Edward Barton Johnson once had his offices upstairs. *(Denise Shillitoe)*

Nos 10/12 The Grove, 2005. The ornate glass fronts have survived intact, but alcohol and cigars have given way to books and one of the many charity shops in Ilkley. The Dinsdale & Co. name is still preserved in the mosaic floor of the entrances to the two shops. *(Denise Shillitoe)*

Above, right and left: The Grove Picture House, looking east along Back Grove Road, *c.* 1945, and looking north from The Grove, *c.* 1966. The cinema opened on 21 February 1913, with a capacity of 728 people. It was converted from a lecture hall and owned by the Croft family, who were also coal merchants and antique dealers. It was originally called the Picture House, but the name was changed to The Grove Picture House in 1929. Sound was introduced in 1930. It was taken over by the Star Cinema group in 1946. *(Bradford Museums, Galleries and Heritage)*

Right: Site of The Grove Cinema, looking north, 2005. The cinema closed in December 1967 and the Council, which had bought the property, demolished it during the following year. The visitor can now stand on The Grove and see down the access road to the central car park and South Hawksworth Street. *(Denise Shillitoe)*

Top: Old cottage on Green Lane, *c.* 1867. Together with Hartley's farm, this cottage was the only other building on Green Lane before the expansion of the town in the 1870s. It was one of the last thatched cottages in the town. Ling and heather from the moor formed the local thatching materials. (*Bradford Museums, Galleries and Heritage*)

Centre: The Grove, looking east, *c.* 1905. The old cottage was replaced by four houses and shops built by the Dean Brothers in 1891. These can be seen in the foreground. One of the shops was occupied by the Kiosk Coffee Stores, which won a gold medal for coffee-roasting at the International Grocery Exhibition in London in 1897. The tradition of fine coffee continues, as the shop is now the home of Betty's Café. The block of shops beyond was built in 1877. Originally all the shops had railings where retailers displayed their wares. The railings in the picture belong to Mr Barron, a glass and china dealer. Despite the inconvenience they caused to pedestrians he refused to remove them and they did not disappear until the 1920s. (*Denise Shillitoe*)

Bottom: The Grove, looking east, 2005. The main change is the large amount of traffic to be seen. This causes heated local discussion as to whether the street should be pedestrianised. The pavement area was renovated in 2004 and the Council preserved the demarcation of the shops' original boundary by a line of coloured pavers that runs the length of the pavement. (*Denise Shillitoe*)

Top: Ilkley Hospital and Convalescent Home. The hospital was built in 1862 in the Scottish baronial style. It was built as a subscription hospital, set up by the Ilkley Bath Charity to provide better accommodation for the poor people of the surrounding towns so they could come to Ilkley to benefit from the town's waters and clean, fresh air. In 1889 an extension designed by C.H. Hargreaves was added. Patients were allowed to stay for up to three weeks and had free treatment and baths. During the First World War it was used as a military hospital, receiving special commendation from the War Office. From left to right, Deaconess College, Wells House and St Margaret's Church can be seen on the hillside above the hospital. *(Denise Shillitoe)*

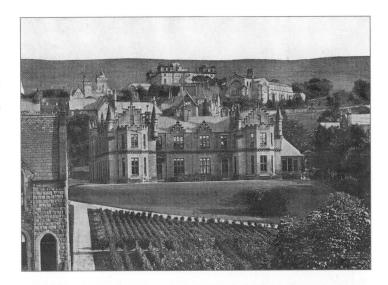

Centre: Ilkley Hospital and Convalescent Home, women's day room. The convalescent home offered comfortable accommodation and nourishing food prepared with fresh vegetables from its own gardens. It also promised 'cosily furnished day rooms, a billiard room and a well stocked library'. Outside there was a croquet lawn, a bowling green and an 18-hole putting green. *(Denise Shillitoe)*

Bottom: Grove House, 2005. The hospital was absorbed into the National Health Service and continued as a convalescent hospital until its closure in 1993. After remaining empty for nearly ten years it was redeveloped as Grove House, part of the Abbeyfield Ilkley Society, which is an organisation caring for older people. The building has been completely remodelled internally. It opened in 2004. *(Alex Cockshott)*

Above left: The Spa Hydropathic Establishment. The spa opened in 1864 as the Grove Hydropathic Establishment. After major alterations and extensions designed by C.H. Hargreaves it reopened as the Spa Hydropathic Establishment in 1884–5. The small building at the side was one of these extensions and functioned as a music room. Exceptionally, the spa had its own spring in its grounds and was the only hydro in Ilkley where the visitor had the benefit of the drinking water without having to climb uphill to the moor. It was slightly cheaper than some of the other hydros. The medicinal department was under a Dr Johnstone and was conducted on 'strictly temperance principles'. *(Denise Shillitoe)*

Above right: Spa Flats, 1988. The building was converted to flats and a café in 1919. Over time the café had different names and owners. First it was the Spa Restaurant, Café and Tea Rooms; then The Bluebird Cafe; and finally Café Konditorei. *(Denise Shillitoe)*

Spa Apartments, 2005. All that remains of the original spa are the gateposts. One can just be seen in the bottom right-hand corner in front of the car. *(Alex Cockshott)*

The high school, Parish Ghyll Road. Designed by Mr Marshall of Leeds, the high school opened in 1869 as a small private boarding and day school for boys. The first principal was Thomas Ingleton. Over the following years the building was extended and a new gymnasium added. By 1881 the school was being run by a Mr Mercer. It closed soon after, probably because of competition from several other schools in Ilkley, especially the Ilkley College. The large spire belongs to the Congregational Church on The Grove. The small one to the right is the spire of the Wesleyan Church on Wells Road. *(Bradford Museums, Galleries and Heritage)*

The high school building, 2005. The building still remains although one of the windows has been converted into an entrance and the property is now flats. Between the first-floor windows on the left can be seen the remains of a date stone. Part of the inscription has been removed, but it still reads 'erected in 1869'. *(Alex Cockshott)*

Memorial Gardens, The Grove, 1953. The cenotaph has 180 names on it and stands 19ft high. It was designed by J.J. Doass, who had won a competition for the best design. It was unveiled in 1922 by Captain Harold Maufe VC (a member of the Brown Muff of Bradford family) and dedicated by the Bishop of Bradford, Mr Perowne. The unfinished building on the left is one of two summer houses that were built to commemorate the dead from the Second World War. The large house in the middle of the picture is Glendair, built during the 1870s for Mr Tunstall. By 1881 Glendair had become a girls' boarding school run by Miss Whittaker, later becoming a Froebelian School. It was converted into flats in the early 1950s. The building behind it was the Wharfedale Creamery, which was demolished in the mid-1960s. At the bottom of the picture can be seen the viaduct which carried the railway over Bolton Bridge Road. *(Denise Shillitoe, Albert Anning)*

Memorial Gardens, 2005. Many of the trees have become mature specimens and much of Glendair is hidden behind the foliage: only the gable is visible. *(Alex Cockshott)*

Grove Road from Spence Garden. The site where Spence Garden now stands was donated to the people of Ilkley in 1895 by Mr Spence of Weston Hall. He made his gift because he was concerned that all the green spaces in Ilkley were being built upon. The garden was planted with many unusual trees and plants. During the 1930s it was illuminated at night. The large house is Brookville, built in 1871 and designed by George Smith. It originally had a spire which was later removed. It has remained in residential use for most of its life although in later years there was a physiotherapist's practice there. George Smith was also involved in designing the pair of semi-detached houses and the row of terraced houses that can also be seen. The area has changed very little, although the trees have grown. *(Sally Gunton)*

Grove Road from Spence Garden, 2005. *(Alex Cockshott)*

Thomas Horsman's shop at the bottom of Wells Road. Thomas Horsman was well established in Ilkley by the 1880s. He was a very successful nurseryman and seed merchant, with nurseries at Rosemount on Grove Road and on Bridge Lane. His shop was at the corner of Wells Road and Station Road. He also had nurseries at Holly Bank in Addingham and at Frizinghall near Bradford. He was a member of Ilkley Urban District Council and became involved with much of the development of Ilkley. This was his downfall, as he became bankrupt in 1902 (along with many of his associates). As a consequence he had to sell Rosemount and his nurseries. His neighbour John Hemingway, a textile merchant who lived at Heathcote, purchased the house and grounds and employed the architect Edwin Lutyens to design a new house for him in 1906. This he did by building on the site of the demolished Rosemount. As well as outbuildings, two cottages and a garage, Lutyens also designed the furniture for the house. The original Heathcote was demolished on completion of the new house. Mrs Hemingway continued to live there after the death of her husband, in 1926, until 1936. It was then purchased by a Mr and Mrs Waddilove. In 1958 the N.G. Bailey Organisation purchased the property for use as their headquarters. *(Bradford Museums, Galleries and Heritage)*

The wedding of William Hutchins to Anne Horsman, daughter of Thomas Horsman, outside Rosemount, 12 September 1899. Thomas Horsman is standing behind the bride and groom. *(Mr Horsman)*

Heathcote viewed from the moor, looking north, *c.* 1908. Myddelton Lodge can be seen in the distance on the hillside and Oak Ghyll halfway down on the right. The Edwin Lutyens-designed Heathcote can be seen in the foreground on the right with the original Heathcote next to it on the left of the photograph. The next house along is Norwood, another house long gone. Next to it is Southern Hay, now known as Glen Rosa, which survives to this day as a Methodist home for the elderly. *(Sally Gunton)*

Heathcote, 2000. Although the house is in private hands, members of Ilkley Civic Society were able to visit the grounds in September 2000 during a heritage open day. *(Denise Shillitoe)*

Advertisement for Ghyll Royd School, *c.* 1920. Designed by William Bakewell of Leeds in 1885 as a hydro, by 1888 Ghyll Royd had become a school. Mr Wooldridge Godby became the headmaster the following year. He ran it so successfully that he was able to buy it in 1903, purchasing more land and building extensions. An old boy of the school was the artist Edward Wadsworth. *(Denise Shillitoe)*

Ghyll Royd School, 1999. Ghyll Royd School moved in 1999 to Greystone Manor, Burley in Wharfedale. This photograph was taken just before the old building was demolished to make way for a new residential development. *(Denise Shillitoe)*

Hollin Grange, 1980. This large private house was built for George Edward Priestman of Beaconholme, Kings Road, in 1911. The architects were Empsall and Clarkson of Bradford. This photograph is taken from Grove Road, looking north over the valley. Myddelton Lodge can be seen in the distance. The house and adjacent bungalow were demolished and a residential estate known as Badger Close built in the grounds. The modern photograph is taken from the same position in 2005. *(Ilkley Civic Society)*

Junction of Grove Road and Beverley Rise. *(Alex Cockshott)*

Hebers Ghyll, *c.* 1910. This area of woodland was leased to the Local Board in 1887 from the owner, Mr Middelton. Footpaths and bridges were laid out to make the stream and woodland more accessible. The board were able to purchase the land in 1893 along with the access rights to Ilkley Moor. The rustic bridges and entrance gate were renewed after the flood in July 1900. *(Denise Shillitoe)*

Hebers Ghyll, 2005. The fancy entrance and bridges have long vanished, being replaced by more solid, utilitarian structures. The ghyll is still open to the public and is a popular route for a walk up to the moors. *(Alex Cockshott)*

6

Westwood &
The Riddings

Taking the waters at Hebers Ghyll. A chalybeate spring was discovered in 1883 near
the top of Hebers Ghyll, originally called Black Beck. The public could drink from a
metal cup. A shelter was available behind. *(Denise Shillitoe)*

Semon Home, *c.* 1910. The home was built by Bradford Councillor Charles Semon on a 6-acre site on the moor edge as a convalescent home for workers to rest, breathe fresh air and benefit from 'kind treatment'. It was designed by George Smith, with separate floors for men and women. The imposing building cost £12,000. In 1876 Semon presented the home to Bradford Corporation with an endowment of £3,000. *(Denise Shillitoe)*

Westwood Rise, 2005. By the 1980s Semon Home had become an old people's home but in 1992 Bradford Council claimed that repairs would cost over £600,000 so the home closed and the thirty-nine residents were rehoused. There was a campaign to save the building, but by 1995 it had been demolished and Victor Homes built the Westwood Rise estate. *(Alex Cockshott)*

The Grove Bookshop

10 The Grove, Ilkley,
West Yorkshire, LS29 9EG
Tel: 01943 609335 (books)
Tel: 01943 817301 (music)
Fax: 01943 817086

We can order any British book
in print, many for next day delivery

*

Specialist Music Department
selling CDs & sheet music

*

www.grovebookshop.com

Hilltop and guest group. This land was sold by William Middelton in 1872. It included a thatched hilltop farm cottage which was occupied in 1877 by Joseph Farrar, a quarryman on Westwood. In 1888 he added a cowshed and tearoom. In the 1890s he had a new house built to a design by the Leeds architect James Atkinson. Its boundary walls were washed away by moor floods in 1900. By 1901 the Committee of the Leeds Work People's Hospital had acquired it and made additions, including a drying room and toilets. In 1908 a boot room for the active visitors walking over the moorland was added. *(Denise Shillitoe)*

Hilltop from the moor, 2005. Before it was demolished in the 1980s, Hilltop was used as accommodation for Vietnamese refugees. The black-and-white gabled house visible on the left of the top picture still stands opposite the top of Queens Road, beside a group of houses built in the 1990s which retain the name Hilltop. *(Alex Cockshott)*

Ilkley Moor Golf Club. In 1890 local businessmen leased land from Charles Middelton and formed the Ilkley Golf Club on the moor edge. In 1893 the Local Board purchased the moors and manorial rights from Mr Middelton. It demanded a much higher rent and so the golf club moved to its current site by the river, taking the original clubhouse with it. The moorside golf course was handed on to local tradesmen and workmen as the Olicana Golf Club. From 1905 it was called the Ilkley Moor Golf Club. This clubhouse opened in April 1907. It was chopped up for firewood after the First World War. Then a nearby house was used as the clubhouse until the golf club was wound up in 1939. Traces of the greens and elevated tees can still be seen on the moor. *(Denise Shillitoe)*

Fern Nook from the moor. This house at the junction of Keighley Gate and Westwood was built in the 1880s for William Hartley. It was extended several times. The view across Ilkley has been obscured by the growth of the many trees planted by the Local Board and neighbouring residents. *(Denise Shillitoe)*

Westwood Lodge, late 1940s. George Smith designed the house in 1872, with an impressive hall window of decorated glass. By 1875 Leonard Horner lived here and added the stable, now Orchard Cottage. Bradford wool man Edward Briggs made additions to the house, including the gallery for his art collection in the 1890s. During the Second World War the building was a refugee centre. In 1945 the Leeds Work People's Hospital Committee bought the house and moved in from the smaller Crossbeck House. The motorcoach belonged to the home and was used for excursions. *(Sally Gunton)*

Westwood Lodge, 2005. In 1956 Westwood Lodge became part of Ilkley College and the Student Union was located here for some years. In 1989 Bradford MDC converted it into Glenmoor Training Centre. It was bought by the present owners in 1999, who made it into a family home with holiday cottages. The gallery has been converted into an award-winning holiday apartment with access for disabled people. *(Alex Cockshott)*

Oaklands House and grounds, and group of girls, 1930s. In 1876 Matthew Todd had this grand ten-bedroomed house built on Queens Drive. It was designed by the Bradford architects Milnes and France. By the early 1900s the Misses Lawrence had moved their girls' school here from Tarn House. Through the 1920s and '30s Miss Clague and Miss Perry ran the school, which accommodated sixty boarders in addition to day girls. *(Sally Gunton; Denise Shillitoe)*

Gatepost on Queens Drive, 2005. After Oaklands was demolished, a group of houses replaced it. Only a gatepost remains, at the entrance to Fern Gardens opposite Arden Croft and Briarwood, a pair of semi-detached houses built in 1898 for George Thorpe of Ardenlea. *(Alex Cockshott)*

Oaklands School South House and the hall. Originally called Cherrybanks, the house was absorbed into Oaklands School as the South House with an entrance on to Westwood Drive. In 1943 Mr and Mrs Saville took the school over and made additions. By 1952 the school was advertised as a boarding and day school for girls from age 9. There was a gymnasium and the school encouraged outdoor pursuits such as walking on the moors and tennis. It had its own Brownies and Girl Guides companies. The girls wore a brown uniform decorated with a yellow acorn. *(Denise Shillitoe, Sally Gunton)*

A bedroom. The school closed in 1965, after the death of Mr Saville. It then became part of Moorlands House School. It was demolished in the 1980s and the Oaklands housing estate was built on the site. *(Denise Shillitoe)*

The Railwaymen's Convalescent Home. Designed by T.C. Hope for Bradford draper George Thorpe in 1881, Ardenlea was built in Bradford stone. The main internal feature is a grand hallway with Minton tile floor and plaster pilasters leading to a sweeping staircase. The house has many fine, plastered ceilings and carved decorations. *(Denise Shillitoe)*

The rest-and-writing room; 1924 group. In 1915 Ardenlea opened as the Railwaymen's Convalescent Home, with hotel-like facilities including dining room, billiard room and elegant day rooms. There were other homes in Cheshire and Kent, and employees who subscribed a half penny per week could stay at them. *(Denise Shillitoe)*

Ardenlea from Queens Drive; Thorpe Hall, 2005. Ardenlea was extended again in 1963 when it became Ardenlea Nursing Home, part of the Marie Curie Memorial Foundation. It accommodated thirty-seven patients in shared rooms. Part of the grounds and the servant cottages were later sold. The home closed after the foundation built a new hospital in Bradford. The building was converted to apartments in 2003 and renamed Thorpe Hall after the first owner of Ardenlea. *(Denise Shillitoe; Alex Cockshott)*

Woodbank. This is an etching of the first Woodbank, designed in 1869 by Leeds architect Thomas Ambler for a house on a 3-acre site with panoramic views over the Wharfe valley. It was built for Thomas Parkinson Muff, a draper who ran a large department store, Brown and Muff's, in Bradford with his brother-in-law. The house was decorated with fine stained glass and had large terraced gardens. In 1909 the Muff family announced they were reverting to the original form of their name – Maufe. It was remarked: *In Bradford, Muff was good enough/But by the banks of the Wharfe they became Maufe.* Subsequently Jabez Dobson of Craiglands Hotel and his daughter lived here. *(Bradford Central Library Local Studies)*

Woodbank, 2005. The Victorian house was demolished and the gardens reduced to make way in 1947 for the present house designed by the architect Mr A. Sykes. The original wooden front door and a stained-glass window were reused. The lower gates from Woodbank are on Princess Road. *(Alex Cockshott)*

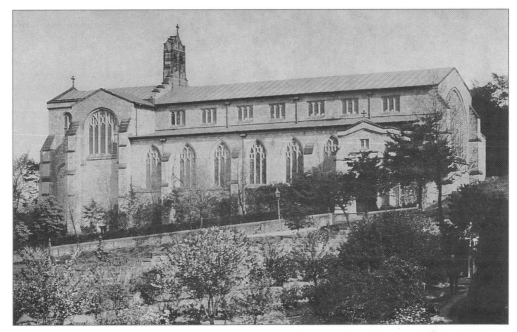

St Margaret's Church, *c.* 1916 and 2005. As Ilkley grew, another church was needed. The later-renowned architect Norman Shaw was employed to design a church on a site in The Riddings given by the Lord of the Manor William Middelton. The original design included a tower, but after a site visit Shaw decided that would be too heavy. St Margaret's introduced 'high church' traditions to Ilkley, including a robed male choir. Norman Shaw continued his interest in the church. He designed the west window, representing the Creation, and the east window. The two windows were made by Powell and Sons of Whitefriars in London and cost £1,500. They were installed to celebrate Queen Victoria's Diamond Jubilee in 1897. The park was laid out at the same time. *(Denise Shillitoe; Alex Cockshott)*

Deaconess College. Originally this was designed by T.C. Hope as Ilkley College, a school for boys. It opened in 1869. Its principal Edward Sewell had taught at the Moravian School in Fulneck, Pudsey. The school with its Elizabethan style and Norman battlemented clock tower took forty pupils aged from 7 to 17. It was described as 'replete with every modern appliance and convenience for carrying on a middle class school'. It was emphasised that each pupil had his own bed. Subsequently a gymnasium, library, museum and dormitories were added. The school closed in 1898 when the owner at that time became bankrupt. *(Denise Shillitoe)*

Dining room, Deaconess College; Deaconess Court, 2005. In 1902 the building reopened as Deaconess College under the Revd T. Bowman Stephenson, founder of National Children's Homes. Women trained as deaconesses in evangelical work to support families. The college closed in 1968, when it was converted into flats and renamed Deaconess Court. *(Denise Shillitoe; Alex Cockshott)*

Friends Meeting House. In the 1860s the Friends were meeting at a room in Wells Terrace. They then bought land on Queens Road to build the Meeting House. Subscriptions of some £1,200 were raised to cover the cost of the building, which was designed by Maxwell and Tuke of Bury and Bradford. A 'rearing feast' was held for the contractors and workmen, who were presented with a copy of the New Testament. The Meeting House opened in 1869. It could accommodate 200 people in the meeting room and gallery. *(Denise Shillitoe)*

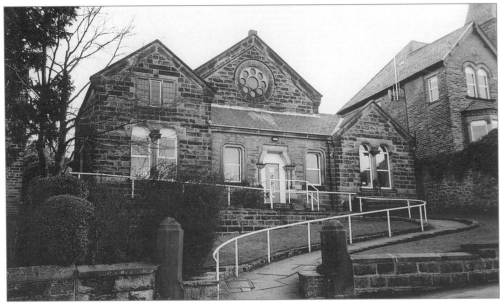

Friends Meeting House, 2005. The Friends continue to meet here, though the building has been altered and extended. It is also used for community meetings and for a long-established preschool playgroup. On the right is Albert House, built in the 1870s and now part of Deaconess Court. *(Alex Cockshott)*

7

Wells Road

West View and Mill Pond, *c.* 1867. West View is the row of houses. Development here started in the 1820s. Groups of houses were built intermittently and one further pair of semi-detached houses was built in 1868, after this photograph was taken. The houses were privately owned and many took in paying guests. The top house in the block of three in the centre of the picture belonged to John Milner & Sons, photographer. The large expanse of water was the mill pond, which served two corn mills on Mill Ghyll. The mill pond was drained and in 1871 a pair of semi-detached houses was built by Marshall Hainsworth, an Ilkley builder. *(Denise Shillitoe)*

Bottom of Wells Road, 1890s. Here were the shops of Thomas Horsman & Son, nurseryman and florist, and John Green, coal and coke merchant. They were demolished in 1904, although the houses behind survive. The building on the right was built in 1870 of cream Tadcaster brick. In the 1890s it was a confectioner's, run by Misses Roundall and Blackburn. *(Bradford Museums, Galleries and Heritage)*

Bottom of Wells Road, 2005. In 1905 the York City & County Banking Co. had new premises built on the site of the shops in the previous picture. It moved here from 46, The Grove. The building has remained a bank, although the name has undergone several changes. In 1922 it was the London Joint City & Midland Bank and by 1936 it had become the Midland Bank, which it remained until it was taken over by HSBC. The building on the right has been converted into one property. *(Denise Shillitoe)*

Wells Road, looking north during the winter, 1933. The shop on the right, built in 1898, belonged to Jesse Bontoft, who was one of the leading photographers in Ilkley for over fifty years. As well as recording the changes taking place in Ilkley, his studio offered facilities for portraiture and picture framing. The open space next to his shop (behind the railings) was used for keeping donkeys, which were used as transport around the town. The mounting steps were later moved and now stand at the junction of Wells Road and Queens Road. (*Bradford Art Galleries and Museum*)

Wells Road, looking north, 2005. A Christian Science church was built on the field and opened in 1941. The block of flats on the left side of the picture is Guardian Court, built in 1974 on the site of the Wesleyan Chapel. (*Denise Shillitoe*)

Mrs Down's Cottage, 1867. This cottage on Wells Road shows the type of thatched cottage that was common in Ilkley before the first wave of expansion and development in the 1870s. Mrs Down, like many others in the town, let rooms to visitors. *(Denise Shillitoe)*

Royal Hotel, 1913. This hotel opened in 1871 near the site of the upper corn mill. Its proprietor Mr Hezikiah Dobson had previously been an ale and porter merchant. An extension was added in 1892. In its prime it had a reputation for good food and wine. During the Second World War it was very popular with the many officers that were stationed in Ilkley. It remained a hotel until it was demolished in the 1960s. *(Denise Shillitoe)*

Wells Court, 2005. Built on the site of the Royal Hotel, these flats were considered to be state of the art. In the 1960s there were several plans to build high-rise flats of up to twelve storeys. Wells Court was one of the few plans that was executed. The height was reduced to six from the twelve storeys originally planned. *(Alex Cockshott)*

Right: High School for Girls, Wells Road. The High School moved here shortly after the turn of the century from its previous location at Holme Lea on Queens Road. The Headmistress was Miss Ida May and she was helped by her assistant Miss Hewitt. The house had originally been built for Major John Middelton in 1888 as Laurel House. It had ten bedrooms with three reception rooms and a billiard room. After the major's death in 1891 it became the home of Dr Thomas Johnstone, the medical officer for many of the hydros and hospitals in the town. He renamed it Annandale. *(Sally Gunton)*

Below: High School for Girls, Empire Day. *(Denise Shillitoe)*

Annandale, 2005. By 1919 the school had closed and Annandale was being run as a private hotel by Mr H.R. Briggs, previously of the Royal Hotel. After 1945 it was occupied by the British Legion. The house has been demolished apart from the façade, which has been incorporated into the town houses built on the site. *(Denise Shillitoe)*

Crescent House, West View, *c.* 1900. Crescent House on West View was a boarding house for many years. It was run by Sarah Beanlands and after her death in 1893 it continued as a boarding establishment. Its advertisements featured its situation on the moors and its extensive views. Since the 1980s it has been Rombalds Hotel. *(Denise Shillitoe)*

Rombalds Hotel, West View, 2005. *(Denise Shillitoe)*

Crossbeck House. Many of the large buildings in Ilkley have undergone changes in usage over the years according to economic and social conditions. Crossbeck House is a case in point. It was built as a hydro in 1861, but quite soon afterwards it became a boarding school for young ladies run by Miss Martha Ward. By 1877 it had become the Ilkley Collegiate School, run by William Watson and his family. Fifteen years later Fanny and Marian Patterson took the school over as Crossbeck House High School for Girls. As well as offering academic studies, it paid 'every attention to the health and physical culture of the pupils'. The house was described as 'situated in one of the healthiest parts of the town, with tennis courts and grounds opening straight onto the moors'. The school continued until Fanny Patterson died in 1914. (*Denise Shillitoe*)

Crossbeck House, *c.* 1925. By 1922 Crossbeck House was owned by the Leeds Work People's Hospital Fund and was run as a convalescent home for women. After the Second World War the house was sold and divided into flats. Having undergone a recent refurbishment, it remains in multiple occupancy. (*Denise Shillitoe*)

Skating on the Tarn. The Tarn was created from Craig Dam, a natural pond on the moor, between 1873 and 1875. Paths were laid out and bands and pierrots performed during the summer season. In the winter it became a popular place to go skating. The large house on the right is the Troutbeck Hotel. Crossbeck House is the end house on the left of the row of houses visible on the skyline at the top of the picture. *(Denise Shillitoe)*

Cooper's Tarn pierrots, Ilkley. Mr Cooper was the landlord of the North View Hotel in Station Road. Every summer he organised a group of players to perform at the Tarn. They can be seen performing *In my Little Canoe. (Denise Shillitoe)*

Top: Hainsworth's Pond and Wells Terrace. Hainsworth's Pond is just past Crossbeck Road on Wells Road. It was named after Marshall Hainsworth, who had a lodging house in Wells Terrace (the house on the right). It was here in October 1859 that Charles Darwin and his family rented an apartment, after Darwin had come to Ilkley hoping to avoid publicity in advance of the publication of his book *The Origin of Species.* The houses to the left of Wells Terrace are known as South View and were lodging houses. *(Denise Shillitoe)*

Centre: Hainsworth's Pond, a popular place for children to paddle. *(Denise Shillitoe)*

Bottom: Paddling Pool, 2005. Wells Terrace continued offering apartments to rent until 1950, although it was then known as Hill Side and St Winifred's. In 1950 it became St Winifred's Maternity Hospital and in 1964 appointed the first black matron in the country, Daphne Steele. The hospital closed in 1971 and the building became part of Ilkley and Bradford College, which was based at Wells House. The building has been converted into apartments and is now known as Hillside. *(Denise Shillitoe)*

Above left: White Wells, Ilkley Moor. Ilkley was known as a spa even before the coming of hydropathy to the town. Although White Wells is sometimes referred to as the Roman Baths, it is doubtful that the Romans ever used them. White Wells opened at the end of the seventeenth century and was enlarged in 1791 by William Middelton. There were two baths, both promising a cure for all ills. The water was cold (40°F) and pure, and unlike the chalybeate wells (such as those at Harrogate) there are no natural chemicals in the water. In addition to the baths there was a drinking fountain at the back, which is still used. *Above right*: Drinking fountain, 2005. *(Denise Shillitoe)*

Old Roman well, White Wells. *(Denise Shillitoe)*

White Wells and Ilkley Moor, *c.* 1918. A charge was made for bathing and taking the waters. In 1829 a second bath house was built for the Bath Charity so the poor could also benefit from the waters. This later became the public toilets. In 2005 White Wells remains an icon of Ilkley, although plunging into the cold water occurs only on special occasions, such as New Year's Day and Yorkshire Day (1 August). The bath in the right-hand wing has been covered, but the other can be viewed at weekends. *(Alex Cockshott)*

White Wells, 2005. *(Denise Shillitoe)*

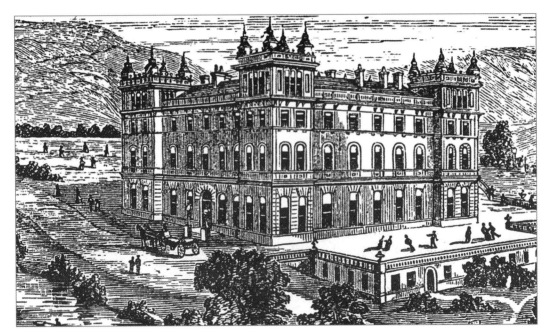

Wells House Hydro, *c.* 1856. Wells House opened in May 1856 having been designed by Cuthbert Broderick, the architect who had designed Leeds Town Hall. The grounds were laid out by Joshua Major, who had designed parks in Manchester. It had 87 bedrooms and could provide accommodation for 160 visitors. A skating rink was built on the east side of the hydro. *(Denise Shillitoe)*

Wells House Hotel and annex, *c.* 1910. The popularity of the water cure declined after the 1880s and Wells House became a hotel. The building next to the house with the glazed roof is the Winter Garden and the building to the right is the annex which had been built in 1894. During the Second World War the hotel was requisitioned by the Wool Control as a finance, statistics and rationing centre. *(Denise Shillitoe)*

Bradford and Ilkley College, north wing lecture rooms, *c.* 1999. In 1954 Wells House became the College of Housecraft. It became Ilkley College and then the Bradford and Ilkley College. The annex was used as student accommodation and the Winter Gardens became the library. Further extensions were added: this one conceals most of the north face of the building. The college closed in 1999 and the staff and students transferred to Bradford. *(Alex Cockshott)*

North face of Wells House, 2005. After the closure of the college Wells House was converted into apartments and the annex into town houses. All the twentieth-century extensions were demolished, to be replaced with housing. The Winter Gardens were removed and the area returned to a terrace. *(Alex Cockshott)*

Bandstand, West Park, 1914. After Ilkley acquired the moor from the Middelton family, this area was laid out as a small park with paths and rustic bridges. In 1904 the bandstand was built to provide entertainment for visitors. A year later an all-weather shelter was provided for the audience, although everyone retreated to the Winter Gardens if the weather was really bad. The music was usually provided by the Municipal Band twice daily during the season. Performances continued into the 1930s. *(Denise Shillitoe)*

Opening of Darwin Gardens and Millennium Green, 2000. After many years of neglect the area was adopted by the Darwin Gardens and Millennium Green Trust. The gardens were opened in 2000 by the author Jilly Cooper, who grew up in Ilkley. *(Denise Shillitoe)*

8

East Ilkley

Cow and Calf Rocks. The rocks have always been a popular attraction to visitors and residents alike. They offer spectacular views over the valley. The more energetic can try the various scrambles and rock climbs within the quarry. *(Bradford Museums, Galleries and Heritage)*

Railway station, *c.* 1900. The station was built by Israel Thornton on land bought from Sedbergh School. The railway opened in 1865 as a joint venture between the Midland Railway and North Eastern Railway. The arrival of the railway as well as the sale of land by the Middelton family made Ilkley an attractive place for the merchants of Leeds and Bradford to make their homes. Many large houses and villas standing in their own grounds were built in the ensuing years. *(Sally Gunton)*

Shuttleworth's bookstall, Ilkley station, *c.* 1886. This comprehensive display of books, magazines and souvenir ware was to be found at the station bookstall. It belonged to John Shuttleworth, whose main store was in Brook Street. As well as goods there are advertisements for excursions by train, to London, the Isle of Man or Liverpool. By 1901 the bookstall had been taken over by W.H. Smith & Sons. *(Bradford Museums, Galleries and Heritage)*

Old cottages, Station Road, *c.* 1867. This type of cottage would have been a familiar sight in Ilkley in the first half of the nineteenth century. These stood opposite the railway station. *(Bradford Museums, Galleries and Heritage)*

Left: North View Hotel, *c.* 1900. The cottages in the photograph above were demolished to make way for new buildings in 1871. These buildings included the North View Hotel. The first proprietor was Thomas Brogden. In 1901 Christopher Cooper, whose name can be seen above the door, was running it. By 1908 the North View Hotel had changed its name to the Station Hotel. *(Bradford Museums, Galleries and Heritage)*

Right: Station Hotel, Station Road, 2005. *(Denise Shillitoe)*

Tower Buildings and Sedbergh House. The buildings on the right are Sedbergh House and its associated outbuildings. It had originally been known as Bolling Farm. During the latter part of the nineteenth century Edward Hirst Wade lived there. In 1893 his was the first house in Ilkley to have electric lights. The castellated building is Tower Buildings. (*Bradford Museums, Galleries and Heritage*)

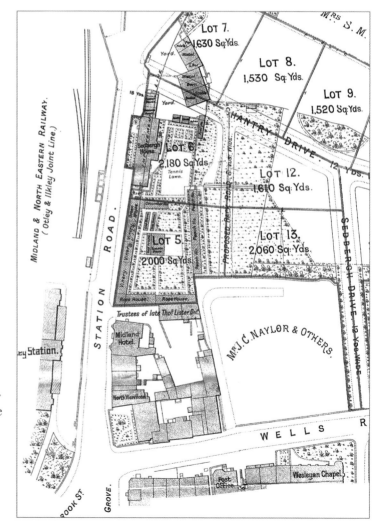

Sale map of Sedbergh House, 1896. After Edward Hirst Wade died, the house was offered for sale. This map shows the property and the extent of the gardens. The site was purchased by John Thomas Jackson, who sold it to the Council in 1897. Initially the Council did nothing with the site except to demolish Sedbergh House and widen Station Road. (*Ilkley Parish Council*)

Town Hall buildings, 1908. By 1906 the foundation stones for the building that houses the library and the Town Hall had been laid. Local contractors were used and the architect was William Bakewell of Leeds. On the left is the library, which was financed with a gift of £3,000 from Dr Andrew Carnegie. The opening ceremony of the library (even though the building was incomplete) was performed by Revd Robert Collyer, the well-known local historian and clergyman, in October 1907, when he was visiting England from America to receive a doctorate from Leeds University. The Town Hall opened in April 1908 with much celebration. The members of the Council walked down The Grove in procession from their former rented premises to the new building. *(Denise Shillitoe)*

Town Hall and railway, *c.* 1960. The Town Hall complex can be seen, with the Winter Gardens that were added in 1913. The small white building in front of the Winter Gardens was a cabmen's shelter. It was moved to Embsay station in 1973 to be used as a ticket office. *(Bradford Museums, Galleries and Heritage)*

ROBINSON & SONS'
ILKLEY
NEW IMPROVED COUCH.

THE "No. 1 A."

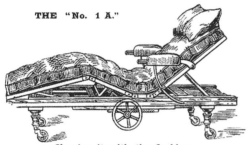

Showing it with the Cushions.

	£	s.	d.
Price in Mahogany, Walnut, or Oak, with Patent India-rubber Hooped Castors, and Arms	12	0	0
Hair Cushion and Feather Pillow in Tick	2	2	0
Rep Covers to do.	1	7	0
Packing Case	0	12	0
	£16	1	0

If with Patent China Bowl Castors, 15/- less; If without Arms, 15/- less.

A Variety of Covers to Cushions can be had, prices as per inside cover of Catalogue.

The Packing Case, if returned carriage paid, will be allowed for.

A New improved Couch, patented March 17, 1885. It has a spring bottom same as the "No. 1," which obtained the highest Prize Gold Medal at the International Health Exhibition, London, 1884, and can now claim, without any equivocation, to be the most excellent Invalid Couch or Drawing-room Lounge in existence.

The Springs are now made from a superior quality of tinned wire.

The advantage of the "No. 1A" Couch is that the back and leg parts can be raised and lowered by turning a hand-wheel made of brass, which is attached on each side of the Couch. The person resting on it, or an attendant, can alter the patient's position with the greatest ease, without any lifting or the slightest disturbance whatever to the invalid, and the movements are very simple, therefore it is not liable to get out of order. And it is obvious that the person being able to alter his or her position for himself or herself, and thereby enabled to take a little gentle exercise without undue exertion, will possess in this Couch an incalculable boon.

It is acknowledged to be the Best and most Perfect Couch in the Universe, and is worthy of all praise that can be given to it.

7

Station Road, *c.* 1965. The Town Hall complex is on the right. Beyond it Tower Buildings stands at the junction of Station Road, Springs Lane and Cowpasture Road. Tower Buildings housed shops with accommodation above. From 1868 until 1908 the main occupants were Robinson & Sons, a firm of cabinetmakers and the makers of invalid furniture including the Ilkley Couch. The business was continued by Hartley & Sons. Tower Buildings was bought by the Council in 1967 in order to make way for a proposed roundabout, petrol station and office block. The scheme was never fulfilled though the building was demolished in 1972. The land was sold and Leconfield House built in 1974. (*Bradford Museum, Galleries and Heritage*)

Advertisement for Robinson & Sons' Ilkley Couch. (*Denise Shillitoe*)

Belle Vue, *c.* 1905. These were some of the earliest terraced houses in Ilkley. The 1841 census recorded that they were occupied by people of independent means. With the expansion of hydropathy they became 'upmarket' boarding and lodging houses. From 1905 to 1930 the first house from the right was the Belle Vue Nursing and Maternity Home. For many years No. 3 (two doors down) was the Ilkley Ladies College, a boarding school for girls run by Miss Milnes. The land in front of Belle Vue came up for sale in 1898. It was rumoured that the Dean Brothers intended to build on it. The Belle Vue inhabitants did not want to have their view spoilt so they clubbed together and bought the land. They then gave it to the people of Ilkley as a small park on condition that it should never be built on. The park is still there, although the paths have disappeared. *(Denise Shillitoe)*

Belle Vue, 2005. *(Alex Cockshott)*

Cowpasture Road, *c.* 1920. This lies on the original path out to grazing land on the edge of the moor, known as the Cow Pastures. The houses on the left were first known as Belgrave Place and were built about 1877, designed by Pate and Dickinson. The house in the foreground on the left was known as Rose Cottage. During snowy weather children tobogganed down Cowpasture Road, gaining great speed and were only slowed by ash thrown on to the roads outside the Town Hall buildings. *(Bradford Museums, Galleries and Heritage)*

Cowpasture Road, 2005.The iron railings have gone, another victim of the wartime appeal for scrap metal. An exception was made in Ilkley for railings near the moor that kept out the sheep. *(Denise Shillitoe)*

Mount Pleasant, *c.* 1920. In the 1841 census occupants of the newly built houses in Mount Pleasant included a magistrate; a hydropathic manager; a painter and gilder; a landed proprietor; a corn dealer; and three lodging housekeepers. The end house nearest Cowpasture Road was added in 1900. Many of the houses let apartments to visitors. The open field in front of this terrace was built on in the 1950s. The house on the right has the unusual name Guise Rock. This semi-detached house was built in 1870 for George Greetham, who used it as a lodging house. *(Denise Shillitoe)*

Mount Pleasant, 2005. *(Alex Cockshott)*

Craiglands, built by Michael Dobson as a hydropathic establishment in 1859, had accommodation for forty guests when it first opened. Over the years it underwent further additions. This picture shows Craiglands after the second addition, which took place in 1874. *(Bradford Museums, Galleries and Heritage)*

Craiglands, 1900. The establishment continued to prosper and further extensions were added in the 1880s, after which it could accommodate over 200 guests. Jabez and Henry Dobson took over from their father with Jabez as manager and Henry as the resident physician. Craiglands offered cold water baths as well as Turkish, Russian and electro-chemical baths. *(Denise Shillitoe)*

Craiglands, *c.* 1900. By 1900 Craiglands had been further extended to provide more bedrooms, a larger dining room, and a ballroom and concert hall where entertainment was provided. There were also tennis courts, a croquet lawn and easy access to the moors. For a while it published its own newspaper. *(Bradford Museums, Galleries and Heritage)*

Craiglands, 2005. Craiglands is the only hydro to have survived as a hotel to the present day. A glass extension has been added to the west side of the building and the ground in front of the building has been converted into a car park. *(Alex Cockshott)*

Top: Troutbeck viewed from Crossbeck Road, *c.* 1900. Troutbeck was built in 1863 as a hydro by Dr Edmund Smith for people of modest means. It had thirty bedrooms, a bowling alley and a croquet lawn. Like Craiglands, it had easy access to the moors. *(Denise Shillitoe)*

Centre: Troutbeck viewed from the moors, *c.* 1920. In common with other hydros in Ilkley, Troutbeck eventually became a hotel. During the First World War men of the Leeds Bantam Battalion were billeted here. In the 1960s well-known pop musicians such as Rod Stewart, Long John Baldry and Alexis Korner performed here. Jimi Hendrix was also booked to play, but the concert was cancelled as too many fans turned up. During the 1970s Prince Charles stayed when he visited Yorkshire for grouse shooting on the Duke of Devonshire's estate nearby. *(Alex Cockshott)*

Bottom: Troutbeck viewed from the moors, 2005. The hotel closed in 1985 and Troutbeck became a nursing home. *(Denise Shillitoe)*

Ilkley Grammar School, 1902. The grammar school opened in 1893 on part of the land once owned by Sedbergh School. It had taken over twenty years since the old grammar school on Skipton Road closed to finance and agree a site for the new building. The school was built by the Dean Brothers to a design of the Bradford and Ilkley architect Charles Henry Hargreaves. Both day pupils and boarders attended the school. It took boys aged from 8 to 17, and cost £4 per term, although several scholarships were offered. Girls were admitted in 1939. The first headmaster was Frederick Swann. *(Denise Shillitoe)*

Above left: Tarn House, *c.* 1892. Designed by the architect George Smith, Tarn House was built in 1873 at the corner of Cowpasture Road and Wheatley Road. In the 1880s it was a girls' boarding school run by the Misses Lawrence. Their advertisements cryptically referred to 'hygienic and sanitary matters' in addition to 'lovely walks on the moor'. In 1896 the school moved to another house known as Oaklands. Tarn House then became a boarding house run by the Revd Mr and Mrs Thomas Hamer. *(Sally Gunton)*

Above right: Corner of Cowpasture Road and Wheatley Road, 2005. Tarn House was demolished in the 1960s and bungalows were built in the grounds. Ilkley Grammar School has been extended over the years as Ilkley has flourished and grown. It is now a comprehensive school, taking pupils from ages 11 to 18. *(Denise Shillitoe)*

Stoney Lea Hydro. This hydro was built in 1883 for Thomas Emmott, who had been a bath man at Ben Rhydding Hydro. Over the years he built additions, including a winter garden and a billiard room. Stoney Lea remained in the Emmott family until 1945, although from the 1930s it became a licensed residential hotel specialising in coach parties. During the 1950s and '60s it was a popular venue for a night out. *(Denise Shillitoe)*

Stoney Lea, 2005. Stoney Lea was demolished in 1981 and has now been replaced with a residential development. *(Alex Cockshott)*

Burnside School. Burnside, on Wheatley Road, was designed by the architect George Smith as a private villa in 1871. In 1877 a Wesleyan boarding school moved there from Selby. Richard Taylor was the principal, assisted by his son Vincent. They immediately applied to have a classroom built in the grounds and in 1882 a refectory with dormitories was built between the house and the classroom. The school offered training for the 'mercantile and professional life' with pupils being prepared for Cambridge and London Universities. The school closed in 1893 after Ilkley Grammar School opened. Vincent Taylor then became an independent tutor in Ilkley. *(Ilkley Library)*

Burnside. Subsequently, the building became a private house and a boarding house. It was later demolished and houses were built in the grounds. All that remains are the gateposts. *(Ilkley Library)*

Site of Burnside and the gateposts, 2005. *(Alex Cockshott)*

Wharfedale School, Ben Rhydding Road. A detached villa designed by the architect George Smith. It was built in 1872 and named The Hills. By the 1880s the Revd Mr Burrows was running Wharfedale School here and had applied to build more classrooms over the next decade. There were lawn tennis courts, a gymnasium and a carpenter's shop. Like Burnside, the school prepared pupils for public schools and university. It later became a private house. The house on the right of the picture is Rydal Mount. The author Jilly Cooper lived here as a child before moving to Ilkley Hall. (*Bradford Museums, Galleries and Heritage*)

Moorfield School, Ben Rhydding Road, 2005. Another change of use saw the building become a school again in 1967, when Moorfield Girls School moved in. Over the years it has been extended and the upper part of the spire has been removed. (*Alex Cockshott*)

Haversham Court, Ben Rhydding Road. Originally known as Eastmoor, this building was another villa designed by George Smith, in 1873. In 1876 it was occupied by Frederick William Fison, a spinner and manufacturer. By 1891 Henry Sutcliffe, a dyer who was also the Chairman of the Bradford Dyers Association, was living here with his wife and six children. The grounds extended north to Clifton Road and east to Lower Constable Road. After Henry Sutcliffe's death several of his daughters continued to live here until the last surviving daughter sold it in the 1950s. It then became a hotel and was renamed Haversham Court. *(Sally Gunton)*

Eastmoor, 2005. After a few years the hotel became a nursing home. The last patient left two years ago and in the autumn of 2005 Eastmoor was demolished to make way for apartments. The stained-glass windows that graced the hallway have been removed, to be preserved and displayed at Cliffe Castle Museum in Keighley. *(Alex Cockshott)*

Quarry. Much of Ilkley was built from the stone on the moors. The top picture shows one of the quarries, while the picture below shows one of the wagons that brought rocks down from the quarries at Hangingstone and the Cow and Calf. The noise from the wagons coming down the hill from the moor laden with stone was a considerable nuisance to the occupants of the houses built on Cowpasture Road. *(Bradford Museums, Galleries and Heritage)*

Ilkley Moor viewed from Cowpasture Road. *(Denise Shillitoe)*

Highfield Residential Hotel. The Highfield Hotel was built in the 1890s, with the additions facing the moor added in 1899. It is at the top of Cowpasture Road, nearly opposite the Cow and Calf Rocks. *(Denise Shillitoe)*

Cow and Calf Hotel, 2005. The name has been changed to the Cow and Calf Hotel. Run for many years by different families, in the 1970s it had a popular discothèque. By 2005 the later additions have been removed to give access to the car park built behind it. *(Alex Cockshott)*

Highfield Children's Holiday Home, *c*. 1914. This building stands just uphill from the Cow and Calf Hotel. The home opened in 1907. Its purpose was to provide a three-week holiday for poor and sick children from Leeds and Bradford. It was open for six months of the year. The ladies of Ilkley provided a parcel of clothes for each child on arrival. When the matron Miss Abbott retired in 1935 after nearly thirty years at the home, she said that over 6,000 children had passed through its doors. The building has been converted into three houses. *(Denise Shillitoe)*

Highfield, 2005. *(Alex Cockshott)*

9

Leeds Road

Queen Victoria's Jubilee Parade on Leeds Road, 1897. (*Bradford Museums, Galleries and Heritage*)

Top: The Star and Wharfedale Inns, *c.* 1900. These stood next to each other at the junction of Brook Street, Church Street and Leeds Road. Their situation forced Church Street to make a dog-leg before continuing along Leeds Road. Both public houses were supplied by the Ilkley Brewery and Aerated Water Company. It was in an upstairs room of the Wharfedale Inn that John Shuttleworth first produced the *Ilkley Gazette* in 1861. Residents and visitors who wanted a drink were spoiled for choice: the Wheat Sheaf Hotel can be seen on the left of the picture and the building on the right with the portico entrance is the Crescent Hotel. (*Bradford Museums, Galleries and Heritage*)

Centre: The new Star Inn. The building of the new bridge and New Brook Street resulted in the Star and Wharfedale Inns being demolished in 1905. The new inn was built behind the Wharfedale on the site of the old gasworks. This photo shows the new Star open for business, with the remains of the old inn adjacent to it. (*Bradford Museums, Galleries and Heritage*)

Bottom: The Star, 2005. The Star and Crescent Hotel remain, but the Wheat Sheaf Hotel has gone. In August 2004 The Star was renamed The Dalesway Hotel. (*Denise Shillitoe*)

Top: Queen Victoria's Diamond Jubilee celebrations, Leeds Road, 22 June 1897. There was a full day of activities to celebrate the Queen's jubilee. There was a parade around the town, ending on the Holmes Fields where a tea was provided for the children and people aged over 60. Between 6p.m. and 9p.m. there were amusements and athletic races and at 10p.m. a grand display of fireworks took place on Ilkley Moor near Wells House. This picture shows the parade on Leeds Road. The man in the light-coloured suit and the rosette is Thomas Horsman. The shop on the left was occupied by T.W. Parratt, tinner, ironmonger and brazier. Next door was George Thompson, confectioner, then in Commerce House were the Barker Brothers, drapers, silk mercers, outfitters and tailors. (*Bradford Museums, Galleries and Heritage*)

Centre: Washeteria, Leeds Road, 2003. The washeteria opened in 1967 and was built into the gap seen in the last picture to the right of the Barker Brothers shop. It was the first self-service laundry in Ilkley. The cost to wash a full load of clothes was *2s 6d* and a tumble dry cost *6d*. (*Denise Shillitoe*)

Bottom: Leeds Road March, 2005. The washeteria has gone and a three-storey building is nearing completion behind the shuttering. It will provide shops with flats above. (*Denise Shillitoe*)

All Saints Church Institute, Leeds Road. All Saints Church raised money in 1899 to build its parish hall on land which had been donated to it. During the First World War the hall was used as a communal kitchen, providing cheap and nutritious meals. It was later used as the dining room for All Saints School, which stood across the road from the institute. The houses to the right of the photograph are in Lower Wellington Road. The house on the left, beyond the institute, was built for the manager of the gas works in 1872. *(Bradford Museums, Galleries and Heritage)*

Operatic House, Leeds Road, 2005. In the 1960s All Saints Church purchased two properties in Church Street to use as a church hall. It sold the Church Institute on Leeds Road to the Operatic Society in 1970. It is used by the society for rehearsals and the rooms are also let for other activities. *(Alex Cockshott)*

Balloon ascent, March 1894. This photograph was taken in the yard belonging to the gasworks in Leeds Road. The gasworks had moved here from its old site behind the old Star Inn in the 1870s. The two men in the balloon are two Ilkley residents, Captain Roberts and Griffith Brewer. The flight lasted about two hours and they landed at Whitkirk, near Leeds. *(Bradford Museums, Galleries and Heritage)*

Booth's car park, 2005. The new gasworks closed in the late 1980s and Booth's super-market was built in the late 1990s. *(Denise Shillitoe)*

All Saints Infant School, 2002. As the population of Ilkley increased an infant school was built in 1894 to relieve the overcrowding in the National school. It was designed by C.H. Hargreaves. Further classrooms were added in subsequent years. *(Michael Shillitoe)*

All Saints Infant School, 2003. The school moved to a new site on Skipton Road in November 2002. The building was demolished in April 2003. In July 2005 the site remains empty, although there are plans to build housing there. *(Michael Shillitoe)*

Ilkley Model Centre. The centre occupied a 'hut' next to the infant school. The hut was built in 1921 as a boot repair shop. The outside of the building is deceptive, as inside there was room for a large stock of model trains, accessories and books. In 2005 the shop lies empty, awaiting demolition when the school site is redeveloped. *(Michael Shillitoe)*

Ilkley Model Shop, 2003. *(Graham Peacock)*

Ilkley Brewery, Brewery Road. The brewery was erected in 1873. It was later owned by the Middlebrook brothers: John Alfred Middlebrook was the manager and his brother Edward L. Middlebrook was the chief brewer. Over the years the brewery expanded and its name changed to the Ilkley Brewery and Aerated Water Company. It produced seltzer water, lemonade and ginger beer in addition to its range of mild ales, Ilkley Beer and Ilkley Extra Stout. A well on the site supplied the water used in the manufacturing process. The company used the trademark 'Olicana', which was moulded into its bottles. In 1874–5 the brewery built nineteen cottages in Brewery Road for its workers. *(Bradford Museums, Galleries and Heritage)*

Spooner Industries Ltd, 2005. The brewery was sold in 1924 and for the next ten years a variety of small companies occupied the site including a joiner, a plasterer and a maker of propelling pencils. In 1935 Spooner Industries Ltd purchased the property. The founder was William Wycliffe Spooner, who lived at Ashbrook on Grove Road. *(Alex Cockshott)*

Fire brigade, Golden Butts Road. The fire brigade in Ilkley first came into existence in 1872, when the Local Board purchased hydrants, hose and 190 yards of piping. The Brewery Manager John Alfred Middlebrook was the superintendent of the fire brigade. He is the older-looking bearded man left of centre in the photograph. This fire station was built in Golden Butts Road in 1894. (*Bradford Museums, Galleries and Heritage*)

Golden Butts Road, 2005. The fire station remained in Golden Butts Road until 1975, when the brigade moved to Valley Drive. The fire station is now a funeral director's. (*Alex Cockshott*)

Ilkley Destructor, Cemetery Road, c. 1940. The destructor was the name given to the incinerator where household rubbish was burnt. It was built in 1905 next to the sewage works at the bottom of what was then Cemetery Road, now Ashlands Road. The destructor closed in 1940, but the sewage works remains in operation. *(Bradford Museums, Galleries and Heritage)*

Sewage works, 2002. *(Denise Shillitoe)*

Gravestones from All Saints churchyard in the cemetery, 2003. In the 1960s the area around All Saints Church was cleared and laid out as grass and gardens. Most of the gravestones in the churchyard were removed and stored at the cemetery. The top picture shows them there nearly forty years later. In 2004, after concerns about their state had been expressed to the Ilkley Parish Council, they were laid out along the wall of the cemetery. Although the inscriptions can once again be read the gravestones are still susceptible to damage. It is hoped that in the near future the stones will be laid out more sympathetically. *(Alex Cockshott)*

Gravestones, 2005. *(Denise Shillitoe)*

Wharfedale Gate public house, Leeds Road, 2002. When the Wheat Sheaf Hotel closed in 1959 the licence was transferred to a new public house, the Wharfedale Gate, on Leeds Road towards Ben Rhydding. Although the Wharfedale Gate prospered initially, it closed in 2002. *(Michael Shillitoe)*

Wharfedale Court and Low Beck. After the Wharfedale Gate was demolished housing was built on the site. *(Denise Shillitoe)*

10

Ben Rhydding

Ladies sitting by the stepping stones at Ben Rhydding. Until the opening of the toll bridge the only way of crossing the River Wharfe at Wheatley (the original name for Ben Rhydding) was either by stepping stones or by boat. The nearest bridges were the Old Bridge at Ilkley, a mile upstream, and the bridge at Otley, 5 miles downstream. The stepping stones are near Wheatley Lane in Ben Rhydding. Many visitors to Ilkley and Ben Rhydding used these stones to get to the villages of Middleton, Denton and Askwith which lie on the north side of the river. *(Bradford Museums, Galleries and Heritage)*

Toll Bridge, Ben Rhydding. The bridge was built in 1882 by Mr D'Arcy Wyvil of Denton Hall for his estate workers. It was leased by Ilkley Council from the Denton Park Estates until they purchased it for £400 in 1948 and made it toll-free. The bridge was sometimes known as the Half Iron Bridge. The small structure at the end of the bridge was the tollbooth. *(Denise Shillitoe and Bradford Museums, Galleries and Heritage)*

Toll Bridge, Ben Rhydding, 2005. The bridge is still used as a way of getting to the north side of the valley from Ben Rhydding. It is only wide enough for traffic to travel in one direction at a time. *(Alex Cockshott)*

Ilkley Road, Ben Rhydding, *c.* 1920. This is the main road into Ilkley, originally part of the Otley to Skipton turnpike. The building on the left was Old Lodge Farm, occupied by the Duell family. They had converted part of the building to Duell's Refreshment Rooms by 1908. In 1934 the Council bought the property and Tom Duell, then aged 84, was evicted. The Council demolished the building to widen the road. They sold the remaining land and by 1936 Ben Rhydding Garage and Engineering Company had premises there, which later became Ross's Garage. *(Sally Gunton)*

Leeds Road, Ben Rhydding, 2005. The car showroom has become a factory shop. *(Denise Shillitoe)*

Entrance to Ben Rhydding station and Wheatley Hall. Wheatley Hall is a seventeenth-century building. It was recorded as having seven fireplaces in the 1664 Hearth Tax Returns, when most local houses had only one. The windows are mullioned and transomed. In the 1840s the hall belonged to the Bolling family, but by the 1850s it had been divided into three cottages. In 1852 John Berry Mawson was living in one of these and the Methodists held their meetings in his kitchen. The station was built in 1865 at the request of Dr Macleod for his guests at Ben Rhydding Hydro. It was originally a wooden structure with a booking office, waiting room and a ladies' waiting room. In 1871 Dr Macleod was allowed to build his own stone building. It was at this time that the small village of Wheatley began to be known as Ben Rhydding. The hydro owned the station until 1885, when it was sold to the railway companies. Today Wheatley Hall has been restored to one house and the station is used by commuters to Leeds and Bradford. *(Denise Shillitoe)*

Wheatley Hall, 2005. *(Denise Shillitoe)*

Bolling Road, *c.* 1920. The first four shops on the left were designed by local architects Baxandall and Critchley for Messrs Beanlands and Hudson in 1897. Ellis Beanlands had his grocery shop in the first of these. The rest of the row was built by John Dawson of Bradford in 1898. The four shops across the road were also designed by Baxandall and Critchley. They were built by the Dean Brothers and have a date stone of 1906. *(Sally Gunton)*

Bolling Road, 2005. *(Denise Shillitoe)*

Ben Rhydding Wesleyan Church. The church was designed by Garside and Pennington of Pontefract and built in 1908–9 on a field called Jack Garth at the bottom of Ben Rhydding Drive on Wheatley Lane. The retired minister from Wheatley Hall, the Revd John Wesley Silcox, was the driving force behind it. In the 1880s the Methodists had purchased a temporary building belonging to St Margaret's Church. This was known as the 'Tin Tabernacle'. After the church opened it was used as a Sunday school and church hall, remaining in use until the new church hall was erected in the 1980s. *(Sally Gunton)*

Ben Rhydding Methodist Church, 2005. *(Denise Shillitoe)*

Wheatley Lane, Ben Rhydding. In the 1840s the only access to Wheatley was up Wheatley Lane from the turnpike road. Above Wheatley Hall the rough road was known as the Raikes. Several seventeenth-century cottages have survived on Wheatley Lane. The houses on the left were begun in the late 1870s. The building with the tower in the middle distance was originally the Cow and Calf, built in 1876 for John Umpleby. By the 1890s, when it was extended, it had become known as the Wheatley Hotel. On the right, the shop on the end of Wheatley Avenue terrace was built by John Dawson in 1899. Moss's stationers became the Ben Rhydding post office. *(Sally Gunton)*

Wheatley Lane, Ben Rhydding, 2005. *(Alex Cockshott)*

Ben Rhydding Hydro. This hydro was situated on the south slope of the moor below the Cow and Calf Rocks. It was opened in 1844 by Hamer Stansfeld, a stuff merchant and former Lord Mayor of Leeds. It was the first purpose-built hydro in England and offered the water treatment to visitors. The first medical superintendent was Dr Rischanek, a physician from Silesia where the cold water cure had begun at Grafenberg. Techniques of applying cold and wet sheets, sweating blankets, baths and douches were used to cure people of a range of illnesses. When the hydro first opened it could accommodate about sixty patients. In 1847 Dr Macleod came to Ben Rhydding and under him the hydro prospered. At its height it could accommodate 160 guests. The estate was laid out with rose beds, tennis courts, a bowling green and a croquet lawn. There was also a gym and a livery stable. It had a farm and orchards, which supplied the hydro with fresh food. *(Denise Shillitoe)*

Ben Rhydding Hydro from the Cow and Calf. After Dr Macleod died in 1875, the hydro was sold several times. In 1885 a golf course was built which can be seen on the right. The small building in the foreground is a lodge, which was built in the 1880s. *(Bradford Museums, Galleries and Heritage)*

Ben Rhydding Hydro. By the turn of the century hydropathy was no longer fashionable and the hydro began to promote itself as a golf hotel. It was modernised and central heating was installed in 1912. Many actors stayed here when they were appearing in Leeds or Bradford, including Gladys Cooper and Raymond Massey. By the 1930s parts of the hotel had been converted to flats. *(Denise Shillitoe)*

Site of Ben Rhydding Hydro, *c.* 1968. During the Second World War the hydro was requisitioned by the Wool Control Centre, at 24 hours' notice. After the war it was not occupied again. It fell into disrepair and was demolished in 1955. The golf course became the Ben Rhydding Golf Club. The lodge and part of the stables were converted into houses. West Brothers of Leeds began building houses at the end of the 1960s. The name only survives today in the name of one of the roads on the estate, Hydro Close, and the name of the area as a whole: Ben Rhydding. *(Bradford Museums, Galleries and Heritage, Hilda Holmes)*

St John's Church, Ben Rhydding, *c.* 1906. From the 1890s, as the population of Ben Rhydding grew, the Revd Dr Muntz held regular services at the hydro. In 1901 a cricket ground at the junction of Bolling Road and Margerison Road was purchased for £650 and a new church was built on the site. It was designed by Cannon and Chorley of Leeds. The church was consecrated in 1905. The first curate, the Revd William E. Bradley, was appointed in 1908. The vestries and tower were added in 1909 and 1910. The tower, which cost £875, was paid for by Mrs Bradley on condition that the parish rooms and vestries be paid for by the parishioners. The clock was presented by Jillah Duell. The total cost of the church was £10,000. It was not until 1912 that Ben Rhydding became a separate parish from Ilkley. *(Denise Shillitoe)*

St John's Church, 2005. *(Alex Cockshott)*

Bolling Road, 2005. This row of fourteen terraced houses was built in 1898 by Taylor and Watkins to a design by Baxandall and Critchley. It is opposite St John's Church. Bolling Road stopped just after these houses but the road was extended a year later, joining with Springs Lane to give another route into Ilkley. The end house was a girls' school run by Miss Wray. In 1928 she married and left the area. The new principal was Miss Owen, who called the school Winton School. In the 1930s it was run by Miss Kirby. It closed in the 1960s, by which time it had become a school for both boys and girls. *(Denise Shillitoe)*

Miss Wray's school. *(Denise Shillitoe)*

ACKNOWLEDGEMENTS

The majority of the photographs have come from our own collections and have been supplemented by the generosity of Bradford Museums, Galleries and Heritage. Photographs have been kindly contributed by Bradford Libraries; Friends of the Manor House; Sally Gunton; Mr Bert Hardisty, courtesy of Mrs E. Hardisty; Mr and Mrs Jim Horsman; Ilkley Civic Society archives; Graham Peacock; and Michael Shillitoe.

Several local facilities have helped. Particular thanks go to Gavin Edwards and the staff of the Ilkley Manor House Art Gallery and Museum; to the staff of Ilkley Library, and to the local studies library of Bradford MDC. We have also spent countless hours researching the late nineteenth-century expansion of Ilkley with the unfailing support and patience of the staff at the Bradford office of the West Yorkshire Archive Service.

Thanks to Paul Anning and Dave Witt of Annings Ilkley Ltd for their help and support and also to Ilkley Parish Council.

Finally, thanks to the many residents of Ilkley who have shared their knowledge of the town and allowed photographs to be taken of their houses.

Middleton Sanatorium. The sanatorium was built during the First World War. Its position on the hillside overlooking Ilkley was thought to be ideal, providing clean, fresh air far from the pollutants of large towns like Leeds and Bradford. It opened with 100 beds, but soon expanded to accommodate 250. It was a tuberculosis (TB) sanatorium until 1949. Then it was renamed as the Middleton Hospital, was absorbed into the National Health Service and became a general hospital. During the 1960s it became a convalescent hospital for older people. It was demolished in 1991. Since then there have been several planning applications for housing. They were unsuccessful and the land has reverted to grass and woodland. (*Denise Shillitoe*)